Kitty, My Rib

Kitty, My Rib

by
E. Jane Mall

Concordia Publishing House — Saint Louis

Copyright 1959 by
Concordia Publishing House
St. Louis, Missouri
Third Printing 1960

Library of Congress Card No. 59-10977

MANUFACTURED IN THE UNITED STATES OF AMERICA

Dedicated with love to my husband,
Carlton H. Mall, Chaplain (Captain),
U. S. Army

Preface

*T*OGETHER, Martin Luther and his wife established the Protestant parsonage. The great number of *Who's Who* personalities who have come from Protestant parsonages indicates the tremendous influence which the parsonage has had.

There are many volumes written about Dr. Martin Luther, the great Reformer. On this great man, what he did, what he said, what he thought, there is an abundance of material. There is, however, little material on his wife, Katharine. Often in my research for KITTY, MY RIB I had to sift through pages and pages of material in order to find one golden nugget — a line about Katharine Luther. In this book I have tried to picture the life and heart of a woman who married a famous man. It is incidental, in this fictionalized biography, that the man she married was Martin Luther.

I wish also to express my gratitude to the Editorial Department of Concordia Publishing House for its help in keeping this book historically accurate.

E. Jane Mall

$\mathcal{T}$HE FADING EVENING SUN reached dusty fingers of light through the high windows of the Nimbschen convent chapel. Twelve nuns stood in a row in front of a massive altar. Their hands were crossed on their breasts, their heads bowed low. Before them stood the abbess of the convent. Her eyes traveled along the row of down-cast heads.

"This is truly heresy," she said.

The row of heads bent a little lower, and the abbess continued. "I have had most of you under my care for the better part of your lives, and you have been obedient nuns. However, this heresy shall not go unpunished. The general of the order was here only a few weeks ago, and I told him in all honesty that this convent was secure against heresy." She stopped and folded her hands. On her face was an expression of deep sadness.

"You know the rules," she said softly; "now go."

The twelve nuns obediently dropped to their knees and crawled to the penitents' bench, where they sat in an attitude of desolation for the remainder of the vesper service.

Katharine von Bora, one of the wayward nuns, looked up once during the service and shivered involuntarily. She remembered back to the first moment when they had dared to hope for freedom. Sister Magdalene, Katharine's aunt, had suggested to the little group that they write to their parents and relatives asking them to release them and take them home. Katharine wrote a letter to her brother Hans, but she did so with little hope that he would respond favorably.

Katharine's mother had died when Katharine was about five. Later her father remarried, and Katharine and her stepmother didn't get along. In those days it was common practice to send poor, helpless females to a convent; so when Katharine was nine, her father sent her to the Nimbschen convent because his sister Magdalene was a nun there and the sister of Katharine's mother was the abbess of the convent, and he felt that these two good women would keep a loving eye on their niece.

Katharine, growing up in the convent, was an obedient nun and never caused any sort of trouble or disturbance among the sisters. However, she finally realized that not their beloved church but a few of the power-grasping people of the church were bringing dishonor and corruption to the holy institution, and it made her long for freedom.

When the nuns heard of the monk Martin Luther and of what he was doing to free the church of the poison that had seeped into it, they saw a ray of hope. Quickly they smuggled letters to their relatives begging them for release from what they felt had become corrupt.

The reply Katharine received from her brother was kind. He told her he would like to help her, but he could not see how a helpless woman who had lived nearly all of her life within the confines of a convent could possibly get along in the outside world. Therefore, he wrote, he felt it would be safer for her to remain in the convent.

The other eleven nuns, who had written similar letters, received answers which were on much the same order. They told one another of the answers they had received, and they would have given up then had not one of the other nuns discovered what they had done and reported them to the abbess. Now they were being punished for their crime of heresy.

For four days the nuns sat in their lonely cells. Once a day bread and water was brought to them.

In her cell Katharine knelt by her cot. "Dear God," she prayed, "grant us a speedy release." She pondered on her sin of heresy but couldn't feel convinced of the severity of the sin. Her narrow cell was gloomy and dark, relieved only by a few colorful pictures of saints. She lighted a lamp, sat down on her cot, and picked up her sewing.

Katharine was not a particularly beautiful person, but her dark eyes, set like glistening jewels in the almost ghostly pallor of her face, gave her an appearance of fragile beauty. She was twenty-four years old, and in her face was character and wisdom. Her small, slim body bent earnestly over her sewing, and her firm chin jutted out as she concentrated on her work.

The heavy door of her cell opened, and another nun stood in the small circle of light. "Sister Katharine," she exclaimed, "did you finish embroidering the altar cloth? It was to be ready for High Mass tomorrow."

Katharine looked up. "Yes, Aunt Magdalene, I finished it." With a sigh she picked up the folds of velvet and handed the cloth to her. "Will you see that the abbess gets it?"

Sister Magdalene held the cloth in her arms. "What's wrong, Katharine?" she asked. "Lately you have been acting so weary and so — so sad."

Katharine's eyes filled with tears. Ashamed, she turned her face toward the cell window and in a small voice said, "I long to be free."

Sister Magdalene drew in her breath. "I know," she said.

Katharine whirled to face her aunt. Her face was flushed, and her eyes shone brightly. "I want to be free from all of this," she said with a vague wave of her hand. "The monk of Wittenberg, Dr. Martin Luther, is preaching justification by faith. Nuns and priests are escaping the confines of convents and monasteries and finding freedom and great happiness in doing the Lord's work."

Magdalene flushed. "You know what you are saying, Katharine?"

"I'm saying that we have a right to choose. I've heard of what Dr. Luther is preaching, and I've read some of his works. They have made me long for freedom as I've never longed for anything in my life."

Magdalene sat on the narrow cot. "Dear Katharine," she said, "how unhappy you are! I didn't realize."

"May I come in?" A young, pretty face peeked into the cell.

Katharine smiled. "Sister Elizabeth, come in, dear."

Elizabeth entered the cell. "What's wrong?" she asked. "You both look so unhappy."

Magdalene beckoned to Elizabeth to sit down. "Our sister Katharine is experiencing terrible tortures of the mind."

Elizabeth looked with concern toward Katharine's bowed head, and Magdalene continued. "It's the work of Dr. Luther, of whom we have all heard. It's what he says concerning —"

"I know, I know," interrupted Elizabeth. "I, too, have heard of him."

Katharine lifted her eyes. "What do you think of him and what he preaches?"

4

Elizabeth glanced at the tips of her shoes. "I don't know," she answered. "I'm puzzled."

Katharine looked at Elizabeth's downcast head. "You are so young," she told her. "You've been in the convent only a short time. I've spent most of my life here. You do not know, as I do, the torture of mind and soul that comes from feeling chained and imprisoned and suffering because you think it is not right to have such feelings." Katharine walked to the window and looked out. "I see the peasants returning from the fields, and my hands itch to bury themselves in the earth and to have the warm sun on my back and the good, tired feeling that comes from having worked all day in the free air. I watch the little children, and my arms ache to hold my own."

Elizabeth had listened to Katharine with wide eyes. "Is that why you long for freedom, Sister Katharine?"

"Of course not," Katharine answered. "My God and my church are the most important things in my life. It's just that the church has become corrupt. Besides, I never had a choice."

Aunt Magdalene smoothed her skirts. "You make me feel as if our lives here in the convent are selfish lives," she said.

"I have been unhappy for some time," Katharine confided, "but I was afraid to admit even to myself the reason for my unhappiness. Now Dr. Luther has shown me that I need have no guilt for feeling as I do."

Elizabeth stood. She straightened her shoulders. "Others are talking about what Dr. Luther is preaching; but look what happened to the twelve of us when we wrote our families."

Katharine nodded. "It looks hopeless. In a few days we'll be pardoned for our great sin, and then I suppose we'll have to stop trying for freedom."

When the twelve nuns were released, they were led to Mass, where they were subjected to the deepest humiliation. With the others Katharine sat stiffly on the penitents' bench. As she crept on her knees to the altar, beat her breast with her fists, and recited the penitential litany, she choked back tears of indignation. The abbess sprinkled holy water over their heads and then lighted incense to dispel the fumes of heresy. "You are again received into the fellowship of God," the abbess announced, and the nuns meekly rose and walked back to their regular places.

Katharine was relieved that it was over. The ritual was familiar, but it didn't hold the intended meaning for her. Mostly she felt pity for the abbess. Katharine knew that this had hurt her deeply and that she didn't understand why Katharine and the other nuns felt as they did.

chapter two

_T_HE MEMORY of the trial and the humiliation quickly faded, but the deep, nagging desire to be free grew in Katharine's heart and would not give her a moment's peace. One day, at the noon meal, Sister Magdalene seated herself beside Katharine. "Do you still long for freedom, dear Katharine?" she asked.

Katharine gasped. "Yes! Oh, yes!"

"Then eat your meal. Afterwards I'll come to your cell. I have a plan."

Katharine finished her meal and hurried to her cell. When Magdalene came in, Katharine ran to her. "What's your plan, Aunt Magdalene, what is it?"

Her aunt pushed her away. "Sit down, and keep your voice low." She looked down the hallway. "You have heard that Dr. Luther is actually helping nuns and monks to freedom, haven't you?"

"Yes," replied Katharine, "of course I have. That's what gives me the courage to —"

"I know, I know. Well, my plan is to write to him for help."

Katharine shook her head. "No, Sister Magdalene," she said, "we can't do that."

"Why can't we?"

"We can't bother Dr. Luther with the desires of twelve poor nuns. He has too much now."

"Nonsense! To him it will not be a bother. He is our only hope. I have talked to the others, and they agree that it's all we have left."

Katharine took her aunt's hands in her own. "Do you think he will help us? Do you think we dare hope?"

"Of course I think so. The rest of you will have to be patient for a time now, and pray."

"How are you going to get a letter to him?"

"Never mind how," Magdalene smiled. "I'll get the letter there. That's the least of my worries."

The bell tolled for prayers. Magdalene kissed her niece on the cheek. "Be patient, Katharine, and pray for us. Pray that Dr. Luther will help us." And with that she quickly left the cell.

Katharine raised her eyes. "God be praised!" she whispered.

The next day Magdalene and Katharine walked in the convent garden. Katharine's eyes shone. "Feel the warm sunshine," she breathed as she stretched out her pale hands.

"Ssh!" Magdalene cautioned as she poked her niece in the ribs. "Control yourself! We don't want to attract any attention."

Puzzled, Katharine walked quietly beside her to where Klaus, the convent gardener, was working.

"Klaus?" Magdalene said.

The gardener jumped to his feet and brushed a dirty hand

across his forehead. "Yes, Sister Magdalene, what do you want?"

After looking over her shoulder to be sure no one was within hearing distance, she said, "Klaus, will you do a favor for me?"

Klaus looked at her with admiration. "I'd do anything for you, Sister Magdalene. You've always been good to me."

"Never mind about that," Magdalene said. "Will you do something very important for me?"

"Anything," Klaus assured her, "anything at all."

Magdalene reached into her pocket. "Here is a letter. It is for Dr. Martin Luther. See that it reaches his hands, for it is most important."

Klaus gasped. Slowly he took the letter. "I have heard," he said, "of what you and Sister Katharine and the others have —"

"Yes," interrupted Magdalene. "Thank you, Klaus." Turning to Katharine, she said briskly, "Come, Sister Katharine, we must get back and prepare the altar for vespers."

As they walked back, Katharine shivered as the late afternoon air penetrated her robes. She felt apprehensive and fearful about the plan, but hopeful too.

That night, alone in her cell, Katharine knelt by her cot. "Dear Father," she prayed, "let us hear from Dr. Luther quickly. If it be Your will, dear Father, only if it be Your will."

One evening some weeks later the nuns of the Nimbschen convent walked in the garden, talking, relaxing a bit before the evening devotions. The quiet, peaceful scene was interrupted when Leonhard Koppe, a merchant from Torgau, entered the garden. He brought wares to sell and bits of news to distribute to the nuns. They crowded around his wagon, eager to come into contact with one from outside the high walls of the convent.

Usually Koppe was cheerful and full of news and gay stories, for he felt sorry for the poor women, who, it seemed to him, were prisoners. Today, however, he was absent-minded and failed to answer their eager questions or smile at their happy chattering. His eyes seemed to search for one particular face. When Magdalene and Katharine walked down the path toward the noisy group, Koppe's eyes lighted. When they reached him, he looked at Magdalene, and she turned quickly from his gaze and grabbed Katharine's arm.

"What is it, Aunt Magdalene?" Katharine asked. "Is anything wrong?"

"No, nothing's wrong. I think, though, that we have an answer from Dr. Luther."

Katharine gasped and held onto Magdalene's arm. "What do you mean?"

Magdalene lowered her voice. "You and the others return to the convent. I'll remain here."

"What are you thinking of?"

Impatiently her aunt replied, "Just do as I ask, Katharine. I'll see you at evening devotions. Now go!"

Katharine's eyes traveled slowly to Koppe, who was still looking at Magdalene. "Yes, we'll go, Sister Magdalene."

As the nuns walked slowly along the garden path, Katharine looked back and saw her aunt receive a packet from Koppe's outstretched hand.

"What's wrong, Sister Magdalene?" a nun whispered during evening devotions that night. "Are you ill?"

Magdalene clutched her rosary tightly and shook her head. Katharine, reciting her rosary, glanced at her aunt's pale face and trembling hands. They looked at each other, and Katharine trembled with anticipation.

Later in her cell Katharine sat on her cot and waited. The door opened finally, and Magdalene rushed in. They fell into each other's arms and stood for a long minute. Finally Magdalene straightened. "It's come," she said. "An answer from Dr. Luther."

"God be praised!" Katharine said. "What does he say?"

Magdalene opened the packet and read: "Dr. Martin greets the twelve sisters and through me, Leonhard Koppe, the merchant of Torgau, will restore them to liberty. Therefore, be ready. On the night before Easter, on the fourth of April, at the hour of ten, I will be under Katharine von Bora's window, whence escape is easiest. Do what is needful to keep the secret, and may the Almighty have mercy on you. Signed, Leonhard Koppe."

Katharine clasped her hands and repeated, "God be praised!"

Magdalene walked to the cell window and peered out. "Yes," she said, "the window of your cell is most suitable. No one will see us from here."

"Isn't Easter eve an unsuitable time?" Katharine asked. "Why?"

"Because of our all-night vigil."

"No," Magdalene countered. "I'm afraid that you're not thinking very clearly, dear niece. Our vigil begins at midnight. From six until then we're allowed to rest in our cells. Koppe comes for us at ten. By that time the abbess should be sound asleep."

Katharine nodded. "Of course. I have no fears now. It will all go as planned."

Magdalene held her niece in her arms. "Of course it will, of course it will." She released Katharine. "I'll go tell the others."

Alone, Katharine knelt beside her cot. "Dear Father, thank You! I know now that it is Your will that we be free. Grant us courage to face the world of which we know so little. Guide and protect us, Good Shepherd, as poor lambs in a wilderness." She made the sign of the cross, rose, and walked to the window. She looked at the trees in the convent garden and saw a bird sitting on the tip of a branch. Presently he spread his wings and soared into the sky. Katharine's eyes followed him until he was a mere speck. "Praise the blessed Dr. Luther," she said aloud, "praise him!"

On the eve before Easter Katharine placed a clean, white linen on the altar and put fresh tapers in the candlesticks. Her shoulders drooped, and she felt exhausted. As she looked at the altar, shining white in readiness for the Easter celebration, she smiled. "Tomorrow morning," she thought, "we celebrate the risen Christ. I wonder where we'll be. On a dusty road somewhere, I suppose." She brushed a hand across her eyes.

"But we'll be free. Wherever we are, we'll be free." The sound of a cough made her start. It was the abbess standing behind her, watching silently.

"The altar is ready, Sister Katharine?" she asked.

"Yes, gracious Abbess. It is ready."

The abbess peered into her face. "You seem quite cheerful, Sister Katharine."

Katharine tried to will any trace of happiness from her face.

"There is a reason, I presume," the abbess said cautiously, "for this elation?"

"Yes, gracious Abbess, there is."

"And that is?" The abbess sounded impatient.

Katharine smiled and glanced toward the altar. "It is because tomorrow we celebrate our freedom."

12

The abbess looked at the altar and smiled confidently. "Of course," she said, "our highest church festival. You have reason to be happy."

"Yes, I do have, gracious Abbess."

The abbess came to Katharine then and placed an arm across her shoulders. "My dear niece," she said, "you are not happy. I know that."

Katharine looked up into her aunt's eyes. "No," she said finally. "I feel —"

"Wait!" the abbess interrupted. "Don't tell me." She smiled, and before she walked away, she said, "I pray for you, dear Katharine. You know that."

Katharine nodded. "I know, gracious Abbess," she answered. "I know that you do."

After evening prayers the nuns walked to the refectory for supper. When Katharine saw the bowls of watery soup, tears came to her eyes. "I am so hungry," she whispered to Magdalene.

"Ssh," her aunt said; "this is our last time of fasting."

Their eyes met knowingly, and Katharine bent her head to the soup.

After the meager supper the nuns went to their cells, where they would be allowed to sleep until midnight. But Katharine sat on the edge of her cot, afraid to lie down lest she fall asleep.

Magdalene entered the cell. "The abbess has retired," she announced. "It's eight o'clock now. The others will come a few minutes before ten."

Katharine took Magdalene's hands. "Go and sleep, dear Aunt Magdalene. You will need strength for what lies ahead."

"And what of you, Katharine? Will you sleep?"

Katharine smiled and glanced toward the window. "No; I'll keep watch. Don't worry about me; I'll be all right."

A few minutes before ten the twelve nuns slipped noiselessly into Katharine's cell. It was crowded in the tiny room, but Katharine had opened the window, and the spring air rushed in, and they were glad to huddle close to one another.

"We are like a herd of cattle," one of the nuns said. Someone giggled, and Magdalene whirled and clamped her hand over the offender's mouth. "Quiet!" she hissed. "In a few short hours you can sing and laugh, but for now we must move with extreme caution."

One of the nuns lifted her pale face to Magdalene. "O Sister Magdalene," she said, "I'm frightened."

Magdalene put a hand on the trembling nun's shoulder. "We're all frightened, but now isn't the time to lose courage." She glanced at the nun's face. "Pray. That will give you strength."

For long minutes there was only the sound of the heavy breathing of the nuns. Then Sister Ave spoke softly into the darkness. "Do you think there's a chance that we'll be caught?" Immediately the nuns stirred, and a low murmuring rippled through the crowded room.

"Hush!" Sister Magdalene said. "We are taking a chance; we all know that. So of course there's a chance that we might be caught." She stopped and looked at the frightened faces which she could barely see in the darkness. "If we act like scared rabbits and lose faith, we most surely will be caught. We must move with caution but also with courage."

Magdalene's stern voice and sensible words had a stabilizing effect on the nuns, and presently the only sound to be heard was their half-whispered prayers.

14

Katharine remained by the window. "Dear God," she prayed silently, "if this be truly Your will, guide and protect us on this perilous journey." She thought of Dr. Luther, whom she had never seen, and wondered what he was like. "He is like a saint, I'm sure," she decided. She felt a curious reluctance to leave the convent in which she had lived since she was a child. "But I must leave it now," she thought fervently, "even though I am afraid, because it has become corrupt and meaningless." She glanced at the sky. The moonlight gently touched her face. "It isn't my beloved church," she continued with her thoughts; "it's certain people in the church — selling indulgences, withholding Holy Scripture, thinking more of their own gain and power than they do of the church."

The faint rumble of wagon wheels interrupted her thoughts. She clenched her fists, and the nuns, in one movement, drew in their breath. The church trumpeter proclaimed the hour to be ten o'clock. They waited in a hushed, anxious silence a few minutes longer, and then Katharine relaxed. "Perhaps I was mistaken," she said. "I thought I heard a wagon, but —" A sharp, metallic sound interrupted her.

"What was that?" one of the nuns asked.

Katharine peered into the darkness. The cold wind pushed ragged clouds across the sky. The trees in the garden bent to the will of the wind. Farther on stood the tall stone wall, a silent sentinel in the night. Again they heard the metallic sound, sharp and clear in the cold night air. "It's he," Katharine said. "It's Koppe. That's his signal. Let's go!"

One by one the nuns scrambled through the window, raced silently across the garden, and climbed the wall with the aid of Koppe and of his nephew and another trusted accomplice. Katharine was the last to leave. Without a backward glance, she followed.

15

As Koppe received them one by one, he quickly suppressed their cries. "The time for rejoicing has not yet come." When Katharine finally jumped down from the wall, he said, "Follow me. Quickly!"

They followed down the road to where he had hidden his wagon. "The wagon's full of herring barrels," he explained. "All of you squeeze in between the barrels and crouch down. Don't make a sound."

The wagon was fairly large, and Koppe had carefully placed the barrels so that there was just enough room for the twelve women. They did as he directed, and after they had squeezed themselves in, the three men covered them with a heavy canvas cloth. The wagon jerked, and they were on their way.

After an hour's travel Katharine's legs ached, and she longed to stretch. Her stomach hurt from lack of food. In spite of the discomfort, however, as she crouched in the smelly darkness, her face shone with happiness. "Freedom at last," she thought.

She was frightened at the prospect of going into a world of which she knew nothing. She thought of marriage and blushed to even think of talking to a man alone. Yes, she was frightened, but a smile slowly crossed her face. "God will take care of me," she thought. "He will protect me."

"Halt! Who goes there?" The gruff voice, amidst the clatter of horses' hoofs, startled the nuns.

"It is only I, Leonhard Koppe, a merchant from Torgau," Leonhard replied in a surly tone. "What do you want?"

"What have you in your wagon?"

Koppe's answer was gruff and impatient. "Herring barrels, and don't detain me; the night air is chilly."

Quickly Magdalene whispered, "Hide your faces!"

Immediately the nuns covered their faces with their black skirts. They felt a refreshing gust of wind as the canvas top was lifted.

"Phew!" the man exclaimed. "Herring is right." The canvas dropped. "Drive on!" The wagon jerked and rumbled on.

A short time later Koppe stopped the horses and lifted the canvas cover. "Three of you are getting out here. You've been notified of this. Whoever you are, make haste!" Obediently three nuns rose and scrambled out. Koppe pointed a finger. "Go to that side road. Your relatives will be there to meet you." Still the three stood in the road looking at the remaining nine women. "We have no time for tearful farewells," Koppe said. "Hurry and be on your way!" Silently the nuns turned and walked away.

Koppe threw the canvas cover over the top of the wagon, and once again they were on their way.

When the first golden rays of dawn streaked across the sky, Koppe halted the wagon. He threw the canvas to the ground and shouted, "It's all right now. We're at Torgau, among friends. You can rest and relax here a day or so before we go on to Wittenberg. We'll go there Tuesday."

The nuns rose and in a burst of joyful and tearful confusion crowded around Koppe, thanking him over and over and over.

Katharine alone remained in the wagon, her slender body rising pathetically from among the herring barrels. She lifted her eyes and held out her outstretched arms. "God be praised," she said, "on this blessed Easter morning!"

Instantly Koppe and the nuns were silent. They raised their faces to Katharine, who folded her hands and closed her eyes.

17

"Dear Father," she prayed in a loud, clear voice, "thank You for granting us our freedom from what we believe has become corrupt. We ask now that You guide and protect us as we journey into the world of which we know so little. Be our Guide and Protector. Amen." In unison, the nuns made the sign of the cross and repeated, "Amen."

In a soft, lovely voice Sister Ave started to sing, "Lord Jesus, be our Shield this day." The others joined her, their voices rising like a heavenly vapor. "To us Thy holy angels send, and let them to our wants attend. Let all that we begin with Thee to Thine own praise accomplished be."

chapter three

WITTENBERG, the new home of Katharine, was an unattractive little town with its muddy, rutted streets and unpainted buildings. Livestock roamed freely through the streets, and garbage lay in heaps by the sides of the roads. Katharine didn't like the looks of the town, but it meant freedom, and so she was happy.

Dr. Luther had received the nine nuns graciously. He had seen to it that they had clothing and a little money. For seven of the nuns he found husbands, and they left with their new protectors to live in other towns. Magdalene, having no desire for marriage, was sent to a couple in another town.

Only Katharine was left in Wittenberg. Professor Philip Reichenbach and his wife Elsa had opened their home and hearts to Katharine, and the transition from convent life was not so painful for her. She worked in the garden, helped with the housework and the meals, and enjoyed the companionship of Elsa. Every morning the three attended the service in Saint Mary's Church, where Dr. Luther did much of the preaching. Katharine felt happy and at peace with God, ready to let Him tell her what to do with her life.

It was now spring in Wittenberg. Katharine straightened from her work in the garden one day and glanced with loving eyes toward the flowering fruit trees. A soft breeze ruffled her skirts gently around her ankles. Absent-mindedly she brushed a hand across her forehead. It was only two months since she had escaped the convent, yet already she was losing her ghostly pallor, and her cheeks, as now, were flushed with color. A finch, raising his voice in cheerful song, flew over her head.

"Hello, friend!" Katharine called to the bird. "Hello there!"

"Hello!" a low voice answered.

She whirled to face Dr. Luther. He stood before her, wearing his monk's habit. The robes hung loosely on his large frame. He was very thin, and his cheeks were pale. His eyes, Katharine noticed, were his most arresting feature. They were large and dark, with black lashes and framed by heavy, dark brows.

"Sister Katharine," he said pleasantly, "I see that you are quickly forgetting your former life."

Katharine blushed and hung her head. "What do you mean, good Sir Doctor?" she asked.

"You have a smudge of dirt across your forehead," he replied.

Confused, Katharine wiped her forehead, making it blacker than before. Dr. Luther laughed and started to speak.

"Pardon me," Katharine interrupted, "I must hurry and prepare the evening meal." Carrying her head high and lifting her skirts slightly, she walked quickly to the house.

As she washed her face and changed her dress, her heart beat furiously. "What must the good doctor think of me!" she muttered to herself. "I become so confused and embarrassed in his presence that I act like an idiot."

Later, in the kitchen, wondering whether or not Dr. Luther had gone, she went to the large oaken door and listened. Dr. Luther was talking to Philip and Elsa. "That Katharine," Luther said, "is proud and haughty!"

"No, doctor, she is not," Philip said. "I believe she's really very shy." He turned to his wife. "Isn't that right, Elsa?"

His wife smiled. "Of course," she answered. "Katharine is very shy. Particularly in your presence, Dr. Luther."

"Perhaps you're right," Luther said. "She just impressed me as being very haughty."

Behind the kitchen door Katharine blushed but remained there listening.

"We want to thank you," Philip said, "for bringing Katharine to us. We're grateful. She's a dear person."

Luther laughed. "When I first suggested it to you, you had many doubts about it working out satisfactorily."

"Yes, we did," Philip said, "but our fears are completely dispelled. At first it was a little uncomfortable because we didn't know how we should treat a runaway nun, and I'm afraid, too, that Katharine was frightened at the prospect of living in a professor's house."

Elsa looked at her husband. "Now we are dear friends," she said. She paused and leaned forward. "We are fine, Dr. Luther, as you see. But what of you? You are working too hard, I think."

Luther ran a hand over his worn, pale face and sighed. "There is much to do," he said.

Philip looked at his wife, and his hand sought hers.

"Why don't you marry?" he asked Luther. "You need a wife to care for you."

Luther smiled. "I have Wolf, my gardener. He takes good care of me. I shall not marry."

"Why not, Doctor?" Elsa asked.

"Would it surprise you if in the near future I died a heretic's death? It would not surprise me. No, I have no plans of marriage for myself. Right now I'm interested in finding a good husband for the poor nun in your kitchen."

"Katharine?" Philip and Elsa echoed together.

"Of course."

"No," Philip said, "we would rather you'd leave Katharine with us."

Dr. Luther leaned forward. "Ah, yes, you'd rather. But how does our runaway nun feel about it? We must not be selfish."

Katharine hurried from behind the door and busied herself in the kitchen. "Marriage!" she thought. "Who would want me for his wife? What man would have me?" She remembered Luther's words, and a smile played across her lips. "The good sir doctor will find a husband for me," she thought as she washed the vegetables.

A few minutes later Luther came into the kitchen. "Mistress Katharine," he said.

Katharine whirled to face him. "Yes, good Sir Doctor?"

His face was stern, but there was a merry twinkle in his eyes. "I see that your face is clean," he said.

Katharine smiled and lowered her head.

"I came in to tell you," he went on, "that other nuns have escaped the Nimbschen convent."

"I'm happy to hear that, Sir Doctor. Who are they, and how did they escape?"

Luther told her their names and added, "It was done in a decent fashion. They wrote to their parents about your escape, and their parents came and got them."

"God be praised!" Katharine said.

Luther walked to the table where she was working, picked up a cleaned piece of raw carrot, and nibbled on it.

"Tell me, Katharine, are you truly happy to be free? Do you ever long for convent life?"

Katharine's eyes shone. "No, good Sir Doctor," she replied, "I do not. I am very happy to be free in God's world. You yourself told me that any service, great or small, is acceptable to God. I want my life in the outside world to be dedicated to Him."

Luther examined her face. "You speak with good sense," he said. "Would you want to be married?"

Katharine lost her confidence and was once again a shy bundle of confusion. She turned to the vegetables and straightened her shoulders. "I haven't given it much thought," she said.

Luther grunted and left the kitchen. As he walked down the road, he muttered, "She is a proud and haughty woman!"

$\mathcal{S}$PRING LEFT Wittenberg and in its wake left a steaming hot summer. Every morning Katharine and the Reichenbachs walked the short distance to the town church where Luther preached.

Katharine worked in the garden and in the kitchen, but she found time for pleasure too. She was very popular with the young people of Wittenberg. They usually met at the home of Philip Melanchthon, who was just twenty-five years old. They formed a Latin class and studied together, and they also gave plays. Katharine enjoyed the fellowship and often joined the group at Philip's home.

One night she met Jerome Baumgaertner there. He was the son of a wealthy family in Nuernberg and had studied at Wittenberg. In 1523 he returned to Wittenberg for a lengthy visit with the Melanchthons. On this particular night the young people had been rehearsing a play and were marveling at the superb acting of Camerarius, when Katharine looked up and saw Jerome standing in the doorway. Their eyes met across the room, and they looked at each other for a long moment.

Jerome was tall and handsome, and Katharine liked him immediately. Slowly, not taking his eyes from her, he walked across the room. "You're Katharine," he said softly.

Katharine was still looking into his eyes. "Yes, I'm Katharine."

"I've heard about you," he said, "and I've been anxious to meet you."

They spent most of the evening talking, getting acquainted with each other.

That night, at home in bed, Katharine lay awake and thought about Jerome. She had never before felt like this about a man. It was wonderful and exciting and a little frightening. She hoped he would stay in Wittenberg and she'd see him often.

Two days later Jerome knocked at the Reichenbach door. Philip answered, and Jerome greeted him with a wide grin. "Good morning, dear Philip," he said, "I thought it was high time I paid you and your dear wife a visit."

Philip, astonished at the surprise visit, didn't speak for a moment. Then he said, "Come in, Jerome. We're glad to see you."

In the living room Jerome crossed and uncrossed his legs and appeared to feel ill at ease.

"With whom are you staying?" Elsa asked.

"With Philip Melanchthon," Jerome replied.

"How is your father? Is he at home in Nuernberg?"

"Yes," Jerome replied, "he is. He's feeling quite well, thank you."

Katharine entered the room, and Elsa noticed that she was dressed in her best and had even tucked a flower in her hair.

"Hello, Mistress Katharine," Jerome said as he jumped to his feet.

Shyly Katharine murmured a greeting. There was an

awkward silence, and then Jerome said, "How do you like it in Wittenberg, Mistress Katharine?"

"As I told you the other night, Wittenberg itself is not a very nice town," she said. "However, I would not exchange it for all the convents in the world."

Jerome slapped his leg. "That's the most clever answer I've ever heard," he said.

Elsa and Philip exchanged glances, and Katharine blushed. Katharine's remark had not been as clever as all that. Philip looked at Katharine and then at Jerome. They were looking at each other as though no one were in the room but themselves.

After a short time Jerome rose to leave. "Will I see you all at the dinner Philip Melanchthon is giving tomorrow?" he asked.

Elsa rose. "Yes, Jerome, we're invited. We'll see you then."

After he had left, Katharine ran to Elsa. "Isn't he handsome?" she said. "I really think he's interested in me."

"I'm very sure that he is," Elsa said as she stroked Katharine's hair. "But I must warn you against him."

"What do you mean?"

"He is a shallow person," Elsa answered. "I'm afraid that in spite of his position and his good looks he is not a man in whom to put your trust."

Tears brimmed in Katharine's eyes. "Why do you say this to me?" she demanded. "Are you afraid that I'll marry and leave you?"

Elsa looked as if Katharine had slapped her. "Katharine! How can you think such a thing?"

Instantly Katharine was sorry. She put her arms around Elsa. "I'm so sorry," she said. "May God forgive me. How could I say such a thing to you who have been my friend and protector! May God forgive me."

Gently Elsa disengaged herself from Katharine's grasp. "We'll forget it, dear," she said softly. "I only thought that I should warn you. I wouldn't like to see you hurt."

At Philip Melanchthon's dinner party Jerome sat next to Katharine, and they talked and laughed like old friends. Elsa and her husband were uneasy but determined to keep quiet.

On the way home Katharine, walking between them, said, "I talked to Dr. Luther tonight after dinner."

"We saw you," Philip said. "What were you and the doctor talking about so earnestly?"

"About Jerome Baumgaertner," Katharine replied.

Elsa and Philip exchanged glances.

"The good doctor approves of Jerome," Katharine said with a wistful smile. "He thinks that Jerome will make someone a good husband."

"The good doctor seems to be as naive as you about such matters," Philip said.

Katharine didn't appear to hear him.

For the next few months Jerome formally courted Katharine.

Then one evening he asked permission to stay and spend a little time with her alone. Katharine glanced at Elsa and Philip. "It will be all right," she said. Elsa and Philip said good night and went upstairs to their room. The light from the fire cast a lovely glow on Jerome's handsome face. Katharine glanced at him briefly. She was afraid to look at him for long. She sat across the room from him and thought that he must surely hear the wild beating of her heart. Then he stood up and walked slowly, purposefully, across the room to her.

"Katharine," he said in a low voice, "do you feel as I do?"

27

Katharine smiled. "I don't know how you feel, Jerome."

"Don't tease me," he said. "You know what I mean."

Katharine remained silent, and Jerome coughed and finally sat down beside her.

"I love you, Katharine," he said. "I think of you day and night, and it's driving me out of my mind."

Katharine looked into his eyes. "I think about you a lot too, Jerome."

He took her in his arms and kissed her. It was a soft, lingering kiss that accelerated the beating of her heart and made her feel weak. When she drew away from him, she slipped a hand into one of his. They sat in silence for a few minutes, and then Jerome spoke. "Do you think that you could be happy with me, dear little Ketha?"

Katharine turned to him. "What kind of life would we lead, Jerome?"

He leaned back and played idly with her fingers as he talked. A faraway smile played at the corners of his mouth. "We'd be free," he said, "to do anything we want to do. We'd live like ordinary people, we'd eat and sleep and work and all that, but in our hearts would be the most wonderful, glorious feeling of freedom. Wild, wonderful freedom."

Katharine looked at him in amazement. "Jerome! From what do you wish to be free? You talk as if you had lived in a convent all your life."

Jerome leaned toward her. His handsome face was serious. "I have never been free. I haven't lived in a convent, but I've never been free. My father tells me what to do, what to think, what to say, how to live. All my life I've dreamed of being free, of doing exactly as I please."

"Why don't you do as you please anyway?" Katharine asked. "You're grown up now. You don't have to do as your father says in everything."

Jerome looked at the floor. "Ketha," he said in a trembling voice, "this is the first time in my life that I've done anything without my father's approval."

"You mean — me?"

"Yes, you. You and I together are going to defy him and find our own freedom. We'll fly into the heavens, you and I." He held her close and whispered into her hair, "Ketha, Ketha, without you I am nothing."

Katharine drew away from him. "Jerome, don't lose me."

His eyes searched hers, but he said nothing.

"Just don't lose me, Jerome," she said again; "don't!"

The next few days were filled with laughter and happiness for Katharine. She walked as though her feet didn't need the ground beneath them. Then one day Jerome came to the house. He entered the kitchen and stood in the doorway looking at her. "Ketha," he said in a small voice, "my father has sent word for me to come home. He says it's urgent."

Katharine bent her head to her work. "He has heard about us?"

"I don't know. Perhaps. This may be something else, you know. Perhaps it's just some business matter he wants to discuss with me."

After a long silence Katharine said, "What are you going to tell your father, Jerome?"

"You mean about us?"

Katharine nodded.

Jerome put his hands into his pockets. "I'll tell him that we are going to be married, of course."

"Do you think he'll approve?"

Jerome looked uncomfortable. "Why are you asking me all these questions, Ketha? Is something worrying you?"

"Jerome, of course I'm worried. I'm frightened. Do you still want that freedom? Do you still want me?"

29

Slowly he covered the distance between them and took her in his arms. He held her close and said, "You know, don't you? This is the first real and final test that I must meet. You know that I, too, am scared. I don't know whether I'm strong enough."

Katharine held him tight. "You're strong enough if you love me enough," she said.

Suddenly he held her at arm's length. "Why don't you come with me?" he said in a bright voice. "We could get Margaret or Elsa or someone to come along and then —"

"No, Jerome. I shall stay here and wait for you to come back to me. It will be better that way. You must do this for yourself."

His face fell. "Yes," he said, "you're right." He took her face in his hands. "I must go now," he said as he looked into her eyes. "Pray that I may be back soon, my little Ketha." He kissed her and walked quickly out of the room.

Katharine looked after him and thought, "I'll pray, Jerome, I'll pray that you come back to me. I'll pray for both of us."

Days passed, and Katharine waited, living for Jerome's return. She felt as if she wouldn't be able to breathe deeply again until she saw him. Then one day she received her answer. The sky had been dark and threatening all that day. Katharine returned in the morning from church and hurried into the kitchen. "It's cold and damp, and it's a miserable day," she muttered.

Elsa looked at her. "What's the matter, dear? Is something troubling you?"

Katharine sighed. "I don't know what's wrong. I feel terrible. It's a bad day."

Elsa laughed. "Sometimes I think that you just can't bear

to see dark clouds in the sky. Do you know that you're cross and irritable every day that the sky isn't clear and the sun shining?"

Katharine managed a weak smile. "I suppose so. I don't like the clouds. They hide the beautiful, warm sun."

Elsa put an arm around Katharine's waist. "You're unhappy, aren't you, dear?"

Katharine nodded. She could hardly keep from crying.

"Is it Jerome? Because you haven't heard from him?"

Katharine wiped her eyes and said, "Yes."

"You're under a nervous strain. I wish you'd get some word from him. It's terribly unfair and selfish of him not to send you some word."

Katharine sniffed and straightened her shoulders. "I shouldn't be so impatient. Jerome is having his problems, I know."

Elsa shrugged her shoulders and went back to her work.

After the noon meal Katharine went to her room. She lay on her bed and stared at the ceiling. What had happened to Jerome? It had been a long time. Why didn't he write? "He'll either come back to me or else I'll never hear from him again," she told herself, and she knew she would understand. Then came the clatter of horses' hoofs outside and the sound of Elsa opening the front door. Her heart raced wildly. Mail! Would there be a message for her? She lay waiting. Presently she heard someone coming up the stairs. She scarcely breathed as Elsa came in and sat down on the edge of her bed.

"I have bad news for you, Katharine."

Katharine didn't move.

"Jerome won't be coming back to Wittenberg."

Still Katharine didn't move or make a sound.

"His father disapproves of his marrying a runaway nun."

Katharine's eyes grew wider as she stared at Elsa.

31

"He is going to be married in a few days to a girl in Nuernberg. It's a match made by the families."

Katharine closed her eyes and remained silent.

"I'm so very sorry, dear," Elsa said. When Katharine didn't reply, she left the room.

Katharine couldn't relax enough to cry. She lay for long moments trying to sort her thoughts. Finally she cried, "Jerome! You lost!" and then the tears began to trickle down her cheeks, and she gave way to them and to her heartache. So much that was within their grasp was lost forever because Jerome had been afraid!

chapter five

A YEAR PASSED, and Katharine forced herself to forget her heartache. In the meantime she had matured and become more accustomed to the world and its ways. By this time, too, she was living in the home of Lucas Cranach, the famous artist, and his wife Barbara.

One morning, as they came out of church together, Katharine asked Cranach, "Did you enjoy Dr. Luther's sermon as much as I did?"

Lucas smiled. "Indeed I did. As always, of course."

"I was surprised to see him in a priest's robe," Katharine said.

"A very becoming change from the monk's habit he's been wearing, don't you think?"

Katharine looked shyly at Lucas. "The good doctor needs a wife," she said.

Lucas sighed. "I know. But he says he won't marry."

"I understand the Elector has offered the Black Convent to him for a parsonage. Do you think he'll accept it?"

"I suppose he will," Lucas answered.

33

"How gloomy for him, alone in that huge place!"

Lucas grinned. "Are you always thinking of others, Katharine? What of you? Are you happy?"

Katharine nodded. "I'm perfectly happy, Lucas. I'm quite content to stay with you and Barbara. However, I'm now faced with a grave decision."

"What is that?"

"Pastor Caspar Glatz wants to marry me."

"Well! He's a fine man. How do you feel about it?"

Katharine looked over Lucas' shoulder. "Here he comes now. I must hurry home to start dinner." She left hurriedly, leaving Lucas puzzled and curious.

When Luther came out of the church, Lucas stopped him. "What's this I hear about our Katharine?" he asked.

Luther smiled. "I suppose you mean about her not wanting to marry Pastor Glatz."

Lucas scratched his head. "Yes," he answered. "What's it all about, Doctor?"

As they walked down the street, Luther told him about it. "I thought Pastor Glatz and Katharine would make a fine couple. He came to me asking for Katharine's hand in marriage. I thought our little nun would be most happy."

"And she wasn't?"

"No. She is not interested in marrying Pastor Glatz." Luther chuckled and added, "I'm coming over now to speak to Katharine about this."

"Don't be too hard on her," Lucas said. "She's grown very dear to me."

"I know," Luther replied, "and to many others. Everyone seems to like our little nun."

"Everyone does like Katharine, Doctor."

As they approached the Cranach home, Luther said, "Katharine has one very grave fault. She is proud and haughty."

Lucas laughed. "You still think that? You don't know our Katharine, Martin. If you did, I think perhaps you yourself would want to marry her."

"I?" roared Luther. "Indeed not! If I were to marry anyone, which I will not, I would have chosen Ave von Schoenfeld."

"She is married to another."

"I know that," Luther replied. "I found a husband for her, just as I found husbands for most of those poor nuns." He sighed. "Katharine's my problem. I tell you, Lucas, I have no intention of —"

"I know, I know," Lucas interrupted, "but that doesn't stop me from thinking you're making a mistake by not taking a wife."

"Melanchthon doesn't think so. He heartily approves of my not marrying."

In the Cranach home Luther found Katharine in the kitchen. He admonished her in a gentle tone for not accepting Pastor Glatz.

Tears filled her eyes. "I am sorry, good Sir Doctor," she sobbed, "but I do not love Pastor Glatz and cannot marry him. I would rather remain as I am all my life than be married to a man I don't love."

"Are you still grieving over Jerome?"

"No, I am not. My heart is no longer broken."

With a deep sigh Luther placed a hand on her head.

"Dear Katharine," he said, "I shall not persuade you any further to accept Pastor Glatz. We shall leave the matter in God's hands."

Katharine raised her eyes to his. "Thank you, Dr. Luther, thank you very much." Then, as she looked into his drawn face, she broke into tears again.

"What's wrong, now?" Luther asked.

"You have so many worries and troubles," she sobbed. "I'm so sorry I disappointed you."

When Luther left the house, he wore a thoughtful frown. "Perhaps," he mumbled to himself, "she isn't so proud and haughty as I thought."

In 1525 the Peasants' War was beginning to reach its climax; there was bitter and violent fighting in many sections. The whole of Germany was threatened with war. For a while Luther tried to ignore the disturbances. He confined himself behind the walls of the Black Cloister and remained there alone for days.

One day he sent for his friend Amsdorf. When Amsdorf entered, he stopped and looked around. The house was in terrible disorder, dark and gloomy with layers of dust over everything. Upstairs in the room that Luther was using Amsdorf found him sitting on the edge of a dirty, mussed bed.

"Martin! What's wrong with you? Are you ill?"

Luther shook his head. "Only ill with worry."

Amsdorf sat down on the bed. "My dear friend," he said softly, "you need a wife. You need someone to care for you. Someone to take care of your bodily needs so that you can be free to carry on the important work of the Christian ministry."

Luther sighed. "I agree. A good Christian wife is essential to a pastor but I —"

"Listen to me," Amsdorf interrupted. "I'm going to tell you something." Luther sat listening. Amsdorf continued. "Do you remember when you tried to make Katharine marry Brother Glatz?"

Luther raised his head. "Well, I did urge her to, but —"

Again Amsdorf interrupted. "I talked to Katharine about it, and she burst into tears and said, 'My heart is cold towards

36

Pastor Glatz. If it were you or Doctor Luther, it would be different.'"

Luther raised his head again and looked at Amsdorf. There was a faint smile on his face. "Katharine, our poor little nun, said that?"

Amsdorf nodded. "She did, Brother Martin." He looked around at the dirty, disorderly room and continued, "I urge you to marry, and I think that Katharine would make an excellent wife." He stopped and waited for an answer.

Presently Luther rose and walked to the window. For some time he stood there, his back to Amsdorf, who finally broke the silence. "Katharine would keep the parsonage clean; she'd prepare good meals for you. Besides, she's an attractive woman, and intelligent too."

Still Luther did not answer. Amsdorf sighed and remained silent, waiting.

In the meantime Katharine thanked God that the Peasants' War might soon be over and that Doctor Luther's life had been spared. She also asked God to bring him peace of mind and happiness. She had been worried about him because he hadn't preached in the church or taught in the university but had remained secluded in the cloister for days. She knew some great problem was troubling him, and she hoped it would soon be solved and he would return to his normal, active life.

Katharine wasn't unhappy, but she wished she could be married. For the most part she tried to put the thought from her mind. She waited on God's will for her life. She felt that He did have a special plan for her and she must be patient and wait until He chose in His own time to reveal it.

One evening she was in the kitchen working when she

heard Luther's voice in the front room. "I've come to see Katharine," she heard him say. He entered the kitchen, and Katharine turned to greet him.

"Katharine," he began, "you know that I'm greatly interested in your welfare. I have tried to find a worthy husband for you."

Katharine hung her head.

"Now I come to beg of you —"

In dismay Katharine bit her lip. "Please, Doctor Luther," she said in a trembling voice. "I am very happy here with the Cranachs, and besides, you said we were to leave this in God's hands. I'm sure —"

"I have not finished," Luther interrupted her. "I am not here to plead for some other man."

Katharine opened her eyes wide. She looked at him and thought, "This can't be!"

"I will soon be forty-two," he continued, "and you are only twenty-six. Yet God has put it into my heart to take a wife, so as to set an example, and He has directed me to you."

Katharine turned pale. "I didn't think I was worthy to be your servant," she said. "You think I'm worthy to be your wife?"

Luther looked uncomfortable. "Will you marry me?"

Katharine nodded. "Yes, I'll be honored to become your wife."

"Then we'll be married tomorrow, June 13th, at the Black Cloister, if that suits you."

"That will be fine."

"I'll invite only a few people," Luther continued, "and it will be a simple ceremony."

Soon afterward he left, telling Katharine he would send someone for her the next day.

In stunned silence Katherine walked to her room. She was to be the wife of the great Doctor Luther! She felt honored, but she couldn't feel the joy and happiness that she thought the occasion demanded. What was wrong with her? Why wasn't she happier? Slowly she walked to the window and looked up at the sky.

She remembered the day in the convent when she had looked out the window and longed for freedom. "What was it I wanted?" she wondered. "Wasn't it this? Isn't this far beyond any dreams or hopes that I had then? Why can't I feel happier than I do?"

Then she remembered the longing that had been in her heart then. She had longed for freedom, but she had also longed for something besides a physical freedom. She had wanted to be like the bird that soared through the sky. When Jerome had taken her in his arms and whispered, "My Ketha, I love you," she had known happiness. She shrugged her shoulders. "I'm being silly," she thought, "Free like a bird, indeed! If Doctor Luther could know my thoughts, he'd change his mind quickly about marrying me!" She turned from the window and sat on the edge of her bed.

Marriage to Doctor Luther! She still found it difficult to believe that he had actually proposed. "Why did I accept so quickly?" she asked herself. "What was it that made me say yes right away?"

Marriage to a great man like Doctor Luther was certainly a far cry from any of her dreams. She realized that being his wife would entail a lot of responsibility. "Now I shall no longer be Katharine, runaway nun; I shall be the wife of the great Doctor Luther," she thought, "and everything that I do or say will reflect upon him. But this must be what God intended for me or He would never have moved the doctor to ask me to marry him. It's like an assignment from God."

She started for the door but stopped for an instant and closed her eyes. She remembered that Doctor Luther had not said he loved her; he had said he was taking a wife so as to

39

set an example. She prayed, "God, keep me humble. Help me to be a good wife to Your servant, Doctor Luther." A smile played in the corners of her mouth. "And perhaps, dear Father," she added, "You can also manage to give me a little love and happiness."

Straightening her shoulders, she went downstairs.

The next evening, June 13, 1525, about five o'clock, the wedding took place. As Luther had promised, it was a simple ceremony with only a few invited guests. Lucas Cranach and his wife substituted for Luther's parents, and only three others were present: Jonas, prior of the Castle Church; Apel, professor of law at the university, and Bugenhagen, town pastor, who officiated at the ceremony. The next morning the same guests partook of a wedding breakfast with the bride and groom.

Katharine moved through the formalities as one in a dream. On the surface she felt happy, but underneath was a sadness that she couldn't explain. She had dreamed of a happy marriage to a young, adoring husband. Now she was the wife of the older, famous Doctor Luther. She fondled her wedding ring. It was a wide silver band exquisitely carved with symbols of Christ's love. Mrs. Martin Luther! In her heart was a feeling of pride and wonder. For a fleeting instant she again wished that there could also be a feeling of joy, but she relinquished the thought immediately.

Seeing Eva Bugenhagen standing alone, she went over to talk with her. Already she liked Eva very much. They were about the same age, and both had married clergymen older than themselves.

"You'll have to help me learn how to be a good pastor's wife, Eva," she said.

Eva laughed. "Dear Katharine, you won't have to have anyone teach you."

"Oh, but I will! I don't have the slightest idea about what I'll be expected to do."

Eva laid a hand on Katharine's arm. "In the first place," she said, "Dr. Luther chose you for his wife. So you can be sure you have the qualifications for a pastor's wife. In the second place," she paused and looked at Katharine — "you're a smart woman, Katharine. You'll get along."

Katharine looked at her, puzzled. Eva laughed. "However," she added, "I'll help you whenever I can."

Katharine smiled her thanks and walked around the room. Presently she stood at a large window facing the street and gazed out. Whenever she looked at the streets of Wittenberg, she felt desolate. She hated the town that was now her home. "Maybe someday," she thought, "we'll be able to leave Wittenberg."

Luther told Katharine he would like to have the public wedding ceremony on the twenty-seventh of June. Katharine agreed listlessly. Luther played idly with his silverware. "I have asked my parents to come," he said.

"Do you think they will?"

"I am praying that they will come."

"Do they disapprove of our marriage too?" she asked.

Luther rose. "I suppose you're thinking of Melanchthon," he said.

Katharine lowered her eyes.

"Melanchthon's feelings about our marriage are not to bother us," he said in a stern voice; "Melanchthon is not God." In a softer voice he added, "My parents are very happy about our marriage."

Katharine blushed. "I, too, will pray that your parents come," she said.

On the twenty-seventh of June Luther and Katharine knelt before an altar bright with flowers and candles. Luther prayed aloud, "Grant me grace to rule my wife and household in Thy fear. Give me wisdom and strength. Amen." Katharine whispered her own private prayer. Soon the ceremony was over, and the reception started.

Katharine walked among the guests, greeting them and being introduced to those she didn't know. Luther came to her. "Come, Katharine," he said, "my parents are here." They walked over to the old couple, and Luther took one of Katharine's hands and placed it in his father's. "Father," he said, "this is your daughter."

The old man looked into Katharine's eyes. A smile creased his lined face. "Now I will gladly die," he said. "Martin, you are my son again, and I am happy."

Katharine kissed him lightly on the cheek and turned to Mrs. Luther. "I will do all I can to be a good wife to your son," she said.

Mrs. Luther nodded happily. "I know you will, my daughter. Now go attend to your guests."

As Katharine wandered about the great room talking to the guests, Barbara Cranach came up and took her arm. "I want to talk to you, Katharine," she said, leading her to a corner of the room. "Tell me, Katharine, are you happy?"

Katharine examined her hands. "I think so."

"What do you mean, you think so? Why, every woman here envies you. You are the great Doctor Luther's wife."

"I know, but —"

"But what?"

"I know that the good sir doctor doesn't love me. You've heard what he said. He —"

Barbara laughed. "Katharine! Be patient! You're his wife now; he'll love you, wait and see."

42

Katharine looked up and saw her husband talking seriously with a group of men. "I hope so," she said.

Leonhard Koppe came to Katharine. "Katharine von Bora," he began; then he laughed, "Pardon me, Katharine Luther. I am so happy for you and the doctor."

"Thank you, Koppe. You've been a dear friend. We owe you so much."

He smiled and cocked his head to one side. "Bah! You owe me nothing. However, if you and the doctor are happy and have a fruitful union, I will consider myself rewarded."

Katharine blushed and excused herself.

chapter six

$\mathcal{T}$HE NEXT FEW DAYS passed quickly. Katharine had been an object of interest before to the citizens of Wittenberg. People had stopped and stared at the runaway nun but had soon accepted her and become used to her. Now she was again a special object of interest. She was the wife of the famous Dr. Martin Luther. However, she didn't have much time to wonder or worry about what people would say. The huge, gloomy parsonage needed her attention. The second floor of the Black Cloister had been converted into living quarters, and Katharine had a lot of work to accomplish.

There was one dark blot on her happiness, and she tried to put it out of her mind. Dr. Luther had not said that he loved her; he simply felt that God had directed him to take a wife. At first this had hurt deeply, but later, when she had given it some thought, she realized how Luther felt. "In time," she finally told herself, "he will love me."

She was also disturbed about Philip Melanchthon's reaction to their marriage. She had liked Philip so much and had enjoyed his company in the days when the young people had congregated at his home. She didn't understand why Philip felt as he did, and it grieved her.

One morning Katharine awoke to find that her husband was up and gone. Embarrassed at having overslept, she dressed hurriedly and went downstairs to the kitchen. As she was eating a solitary breakfast, Wolfgang Sieberger, the gardener and handy man, limped in.

A man of about the same age as Luther, Wolf, as they called him, was lame, and his limp was quite noticeable. His shoulders were stooped from bending to his gardener's work. His hair was unkempt, and he wore a perpetual frown.

Katharine knew that Wolf wasn't happy about having a woman come into the parsonage. He had prided himself for some time on the fact that Dr. Luther couldn't get along without his faithful Wolf to care for him. A wife would take over many of his duties, and Wolf was afraid he would be relegated to a place far in the background; hence he was open in his dislike of Katharine.

"Good morning, Wolf."

Wolf grumbled and started to leave.

"Where's Dr. Luther?" Katharine asked.

"Where he always is at six in the morning," Wolf mumbled.

Irritated by his attitude, Katharine snapped, "And where is that?"

Wolf looked at her and sighed. "In his study," he said, as though he were explaining something to a stupid child.

"Thank you," Katharine said. She didn't feel like arguing with Wolf. She didn't even feel like making an effort to win his friendship. He obviously didn't like her, but she couldn't make herself care. She felt as if she had a big-enough worry making the doctor love her. Also at the moment, she was worrying about the noon meal. She knew there would be students and professors dining with them, and she wondered where she was to get the provisions. She hated to have to ask

Wolf and go through another round of questions and answers with him.

They both started at the knock on the door. Wolf recovered first and started for the door. Katharine rose and in a firm voice said, "I will answer the door, Wolf." He shrugged his shoulders and went out the kitchen door.

At the front door stood a woman with a large basket on her arm.

"Come in," Katharine smiled.

The woman stepped inside. She tugged at the ends of the head scarf she wore. "Mrs. Luther," she said in a shy voice, "I have come to present you —" she faltered and then suddenly thrust the basket at Katharine — "here, — a wedding gift."

Katharine took the basket. "Why, thank you! Thank you so much! Who are you?"

The woman seemed more at ease. "I'm a widow," she replied; "I was all alone and had a hard time getting along. My only son was a monk and couldn't help me. Then the blessed Dr. Luther came along, and my son is home again." Tears filled her eyes. "I have my son again." She squeezed Katharine's hand. "Praise the blessed Dr. Luther," she said, "praise him!" She left suddenly.

Katharine took the basket into the kitchen and lifted the cloth. Inside were eggs and freshly cleaned vegetables and chickens. "God be praised!" she said.

Now that there was no worry about the noon meal, she decided to explore the grounds around the parsonage. In the garden she saw Wolf busy digging. When he saw her coming toward him, he turned his back and dug more furiously around a rosebush. Katharine decided to ignore him and wandered around the garden alone. In her mind she laid out plots for a vegetable garden. She visioned a chicken yard in one corner and lawn furniture under the huge pear tree in the front yard. She walked over to Wolf and addressed his back.

"What are you doing?" she asked pleasantly.

"As you can see," he replied, "I am digging around this bush. I am loosening the dirt."

Katharine ignored his sarcasm and said, "Will you help me lay out a vegetable garden, Wolf?"

"If the doctor says I should."

"I'll talk to the doctor." She hesitated. "Will you be ready to start tomorrow?"

Wolf nodded and kept on digging around the bush.

"What's in those woods across the way, Wolf?" Katharine persisted.

"Trees."

"What else?"

"A pond."

Katharine looked at his stubborn back and sighed. She walked into the woods and came to the little pond and decided that soon she'd try to net some fish.

In the next few weeks Wolf and Katharine worked at getting a vegetable garden started. When it was finished and rows of vegetables had been planted, Katharine looked at it with satisfaction. She visioned the rows of cabbage, melons, radishes, and cucumbers they would have. She was tired, and every muscle in her body ached. She rubbed a hand across her forehead.

Luther came out then, and Katharine waited for him to say something about her garden. She felt sure he would be pleased. He walked up to her and put an arm across her shoulder. "Well, Katharine, what a wonderful garden!"

She smiled. "Yes, Sir Doctor, it is a nice garden."

47

"What will grow in this wonderful garden?"

Katharine's eyes shone. "Oh," she said, "carrots and cabbage and —"

Luther patted her on the shoulder absent-mindedly and walked over to Wolf. "What have we here, Wolf?" he asked.

Wolf straightened. "I'm digging around this rosebush, Doctor. This bush will produce roses such as you have never seen."

Luther smiled. "Wolf, with all the love you give these roses, it's no wonder they're so lovely."

"Yes, Doctor," Wolf smiled.

"Let's go look at the others, Wolf. There should be buds by now." The men strolled away.

Desolately Katharine looked down the neat rows of the garden. Tears came to her eyes, and she impatiently brushed them away. She started for the house. "The good sir doctor can't eat roses," she thought. "He'll be mighty glad when I put cabbage and carrots on his plate this summer instead of roses!" As she walked to the house, Luther turned to ask her to come with him to look at the roses, but she was gone.

That evening Katharine sat in Luther's study and sewed while he worked at his desk. She had made several attempts at conversation, but Luther had only grunted in reply once or twice. On his desk was a small vase of rosebuds, and Katharine avoided looking at them. She glanced at her husband, then quickly looked away. She felt that little by little he was beginning to love her. "The pity he felt for me is deepening into love," she thought.

Again she raised her eyes to Luther, whose leonine head was bent purposefully over the pile of papers on his desk. With an abrupt movement she rose. "I'm through with my sewing," she said aloud. She looked at her husband. His head was still bent to his work. "Good night, Sir Doctor," she said in a small voice. He didn't answer. Slowly she walked to the door. Over her shoulder she cast a look toward Luther, one filled with a longing question. Again, softly now, she said, "Good night, Sir Doctor."

He raised his head and smiled. Abruptly he threw his pen down. "Come here, Katharine," he said in a tired voice.

Shyly she walked toward him, and he rose and took her in his arms. "You are so dear to me," he said, "and I know that I neglect you. Forgive me, dear wife." He kissed the top of her head. "I have so many things to do, so many things that are so important, and I thank God for an understanding wife." He drew back and looked into her eyes. "You do understand, my dear?" he asked.

Katharine returned his gaze and nodded. He drew her close again and said, "Thank you. God surely directed me to you."

Later Katharine prepared for bed with a warm, safe feeling in her heart. In the darkness she smiled. "The good sir doctor loves me," she thought. "He truly loves me."

Each day presented new challenges to Katharine. Slowly, little by little, she felt that she and Dr. Luther were becoming truly one person. His work was all-important, but now once in a while their eyes would meet, and words were unnecessary. She felt loved and protected.

Then one day she heard about some gossip that was stirring through Wittenberg, and she was angry. Very angry. The anger terrified her because it was an emotion she had been trained since childhood to control. She faced her husband. "What can we do about this terrible thing, Doctor?"

49

Luther sighed. "We can do nothing about it, Katharine. When people are saying that after a few weeks of marriage you are brought to bed with a child, what can we say?"

Katharine winced and turned her head.

"They have made up this lie out of nothing," Luther continued. "Time will prove them wrong. You and I know there's no truth to it, so we will have to forget it."

Katharine faced him. Her fists were clenched at her sides. "Why do they say these things?" she demanded. "Why do they persecute us? We've done them no harm."

"Katharine, you will have to bear many such things as long as you're married to me. I have been persecuted, as you put it, for years. Now they can include you in their evil gossip. That's part of your lot as Doctor Martin Luther's wife." He looked away. "I'm sorry," he added.

"They're mean and hateful, and I'll —"

"You will do nothing, Katharine," Luther interrupted, "except to ask God to cleanse your heart from anger toward these simple gossips and perhaps memorize the Thirty-first Psalm. It will give you comfort."

Katharine started to cry. Her thin body shook with the effort to control her anger and tears. "Now you scold me," she sobbed. "Now it's I who am wrong."

Slowly Luther rose and crossed the room. He took her in his arms and put her head on his shoulder. In a strong voice he said, "The devil and the world would have you leave Doctor Luther. But the harder they press you, the more firmly shall I hold you; for here alone is your abiding place." He kissed the top of her head and left the room.

Katharine stood in the spot where Luther had left her. His words rang in her ears. She wiped the tears from her eyes and crossed to the chair by the window. She opened her Bible and began reading the Thirty-first Psalm:

"In Thee, O Lord, do I put my trust; let me never be ashamed; deliver me in Thy righteousness. Bow down Thine ear to me; deliver me speedily; be Thou my strong Rock, for an house of defense to save me. For Thou art my Rock and my Fortress; therefore for Thy name's sake lead me and guide me. Pull me out of the net that they have laid privily for me; for Thou art my Strength. Into Thine hand —"

$\mathcal{T}$HE GOSSIP, with no confirmation, died a natural death as the weeks passed. In the meantime, parsonage life rushed on for the Luthers. An endless stream of unfortunates found their way to the parsonage, and the Luthers shared with them whatever they had. One day, while Katharine was busy in the kitchen, there was a knock on the door, and she hurried to answer it. As she walked down the great hallway, she mumbled to herself, "If only a few hours of the day could pass without a knock on the door! Always it's somebody begging us for money or food or a place to stay. Why in good heaven's name doesn't somebody bring us something once in a while?" She smoothed her apron and opened the door.

A tall, well-dressed man stood before her. "I am Archbishop Albert of Mayence," he announced. "Is the good doctor at home?"

Katharine smiled and opened the door wide. "Come in. I will take you to my husband." She preceded him up the winding stairway to the study, and his voice followed her.

"I am happy to know you, Mrs. Luther, and have come to congratulate the doctor on his fortune in getting a wife."

Katharine stopped at the closed door of the study. She raised her eyes to the archbishop. "Thank you," she said; "but it is really I who am fortunate. God has blessed me with a wonderful husband."

The archbishop smiled and went into Luther's study. Katharine closed the door behind him and went back to the kitchen. In about an hour she heard Luther calling her. She wiped her hands and hastily adjusted the little cap she wore and walked sedately to the study.

"Mrs. Luther," the archbishop said, "I want to give you and the doctor a wedding gift. I didn't know what to buy, so I hope that you will accept this small gift of money." He held out an envelope to her.

Katharine took it and smiled. "Thank you," she said; "you have no idea how much the doctor and I appreciate this —"

"Katharine, return the gift to the archbishop." Luther's voice sounded tired.

"Return it?" Katharine looked at Luther in dismay.

"That's what I said." He turned to the archbishop. "We do appreciate your generous gift, sir, but we cannot accept it. God has a job for me, and I am doing it. I will do it with no help but His. God will provide."

Reluctantly the archbishop accepted the envelope from Katharine. "I, too, am sorry, Doctor Luther," he said, "but I don't understand."

"Because," Luther replied, "the practice of accepting gifts could prove embarrassing for me. Once a bishop I know of sent one of our pastors a piece of damask to induce him to disavow our Gospel; and having succeeded in his object by the gift and by his flatteries, he said everywhere, 'What dreadful knaves these Lutherans are! They'll do anything for money!'"

The archbishop shrugged his shoulders and put the money in his pocket. Katharine said nothing. How badly they needed the money! There was so much going out and so little coming in. She hated to have to turn it down.

When the men had exchanged good-bys, Katharine led their guest to the door and stepped out on the front stoop with him. "I know you'll think I'm bold," she said as she detained him with a hand on his sleeve, "but I will accept the money gladly."

The archbishop raised his eyebrows and looked more closely into her face.

"The doctor accepts students and traveling pastors into our home for bed and board. He never turns down anyone who comes begging for money and food." She cast a shy glance at the archbishop and then looked away. "The doctor is a generous man and a very kind one. He doesn't think he should take the money, but I —"

The archbishop interrupted her with a hearty laugh. "Mrs. Luther, you have a good head on your shoulders. Take the gift, and it will be our secret."

Katharine smiled and took the envelope and again thanked him. When he had gone, she counted the money. There were two hundred and fifty florins. "God be praised!" she said and tucked the enevelope into her apron pocket. As she turned to go into the house, she saw Wolf walking around the side. "I wonder if he saw this," she thought.

Several nights later Katharine was in her room sewing. The night air was warm, and she felt at peace and contented. Luther entered the room and seated himself opposite her. He looked into her eyes with a penetrating gaze.

"Good evening, Doctor," Katharine said and looked at him. He didn't answer. He kept his eyes fixed on hers. Katharine went back to her sewing. Finally she asked uncomfortably, "Is anything wrong, Doctor?"

"I dare say not, Katharine."

She looked at him again, and then he stood in front of her. "I understand," he said, "from a reliable source, that you played quite a trick on me."

Katharine looked up. "I did? I?"

"Yes, you." He leaned down and whispered, "What did you do with the money — the money you accepted from Archbishop Albert?"

Katharine flushed. Her hands stopped their swift sewing, and she stammered, "You — know — about that?"

"Obviously I do."

She looked as if she were going to cry. She wished desperately that she could run.

Abruptly the silence was broken. Luther leaned back and roared with laughter. "My Lord Kate!" he said; "my precious Lord Kate!"

Katharine felt every nerve in her body relax. A slow, tentative smile erased the tension from her face. "You're not angry?"

Luther, still laughing, shook his head.

"You do understand why I did it?"

Luther nodded. "Yes, Lord Kate, I understand," he said and leaned down to kiss her. "I really do understand," he said softly and left the room chuckling.

Katharine leaned back and stared at the door for minutes after he had left the room. Then she picked up her sewing and whispered, "God be praised!"

A few days later Katharine went to the door and found five monks standing before her. They were dirty and unkempt. As she stared, one of them stepped forward.

"Begging your pardon, Mrs. Luther," he said, "we have come to your door in the hope that you will give us a bite to eat."

Katharine frowned. She didn't like their looks. There was something about them that caused her to distrust them. "I'm sorry," she replied; "we have so many to feed and so little —"

She was interrupted by Luther's booming voice. "Come in, come in!" he said and walked to the door. "Katharine, get them food and something to drink."

With a sigh and a shrug of her shoulders Katharine went into the kitchen. She heard Luther escorting the monks into his study. When she brought a tray of food into the study, she found her husband giving the strangers pieces of cloth. She put the tray on a table, and while the monks ate, she spoke to Luther. "Dear Doctor, what in heaven's name are you doing?"

Luther wore an innocent look. "Why, giving them cloth for warm jackets," he replied.

"I don't suppose that we need it!"

"Not as badly as they do."

With an exasperated movement of her hands, Katharine left the room. Presently she heard the monks leave, and she hurried to the study. She stood in the doorway, her hands on her hips. "Dear Doctor," she said in a tight voice, "you made a mistake."

Luther gave her a long look. "We must share what we have, Katharine."

"I still say you made a mistake." She crossed the room. "They were disreputable characters. You would have done better, in my eyes, to have saved your charity for someone more deserving."

Luther bent his head to his desk. "I am more concerned with the eyes of my Lord," he said.

56

In exasperation Katharine left the room. Presently he heard her banging pots and pans in the kitchen. He smiled and continued working.

That night the Luthers had been asleep for several hours when Katharine awoke with a start. She heard voices downstairs. "I suppose," she thought with a yawn, "that the doctor can't sleep and so is practicing tomorrow's sermon." She wanted to roll over and go back to sleep, but the image of her husband wandering sleepless and alone through the great rooms downstairs troubled her, and she rose and slipped into a robe and went downstairs. She entered the study and saw the same monks rummaging through the cupboards. One held a large bag into which the others were dropping everything they could lay their hands on. Katharine stifled a scream with the back of her hand and silently fled up the stairs to her husband's room. "Doctor!" she whispered, "dear Sir Doctor! Wake up quickly!"

Luther awoke and sat up. "Katharine! What's wrong?"

"Those monks are down in your study. They're robbing us."

"Now?"

"Yes, Doctor, now! Right this minute!"

Hurriedly Luther got out of bed, slipped into a robe, and started downstairs. Katharine walked close behind him. Luther threw open the study door and boomed, "What do you think you are doing?"

The thieves dropped their bag and whirled to face Luther. He shouted at them. His booming voice and angry face were more terrible than any weapon. "You came to me asking for food and drink, and I gave it to you and also gave you cloth for jackets." His eyes searched their frightened faces. "Then you come back to me as thieves. Thank God that not all of the runaway monks are like you. Go! Get out of my house! Get out before I take a whip to your backs!"

The men slithered past Luther and ran out of the house. When they were gone, Katharine slumped into a chair.

"You were right, Katharine," Luther said; "they were disreputable characters."

Katharine raised her eyes. "O Doctor," she cried, "I'm so sorry!" and she threw herself into his arms.

He held her close, and his lips brushed the top of her head. "Sorry, dear wife?" he asked, "because you think that I've been betrayed?"

Katharine nodded her head against his chest.

"No, my dear," Luther continued; "they haven't hurt me. They've only hurt themselves." He sighed and ran his fingers through her hair. "I'd do it all over again."

Katharine watched as he took the contents of the thieves' bag and began restoring order to the room. At times like this Luther was tender and understanding, and Katharine cherished these moments, because she still felt as though in many ways she wasn't really a part of Luther's life. They were both absorbed in their work and of necessity had little time together.

Even the mealtime offered no opportunity for them to talk to each other because the table was always surrounded by students and visitors. The discussions at mealtime were nearly always of a theological nature, with Luther talking and the students, wide-eyed, hanging on his every word.

Katharine finally concluded that parsonage life was not conducive to a normal, happy family life. A parsonage couple had to work harder than other married people to remain happy and be close to each other. "But," her eyes twinkled, "we also have the advantage in that we lean heavily on the Lord for our happiness."

When people saw her in the garden at sunup, her small back bent to the job of digging or hoeing, they said, "My, Katharine's such a worker!" And they smiled when they saw her bustling about the great parsonage, cooking, cleaning, and sewing. Sometimes, when she was alone, she laughed. "I've been working and bustling since I was five years old," she thought, "I don't know how to act any other way."

She hardly dared to admit, even to herself, that some of the reason for her constant activity was the desire to stifle the hunger that lay deep in her heart. All her life she had hungered after love and affection. She wanted someone who would caress her and run a loving hand over her brow when she was silent. Someone who cared about the littlest things merely because they happened to her. She had never felt a mother's or a father's love and affection. She had been loved in the convent, but it wasn't the same deep personal love that she longed for. "Someday," she often thought, "the doctor and I will be able to retire from parsonage life, and then we'll have more time for each other."

Now she watched Luther as he restored order to the room. Deep in her heart she felt love for this great man who was her husband.

Just then he paused and looked at her. His dark eyes sparkled as he said, "I love you, dear wife."

Katharine rose and put her hand in his. "Let's straighten the room in the morning, dear Doctor."

Arm in arm they went upstairs.

chapter eight

$\mathcal{T}$HE WEEKS PASSED, and Luther and Katharine were busy as usual. Katharine hadn't seen her Aunt Magdalene since that long-ago day when they had arrived in Wittenberg, runaway nuns. One day she mentioned this to Luther, and he responded immediately, "Would you like for Lena to come live with us, Katharine?"

"Oh, yes, Doctor! She's almost like a mother to me. I would like very much to have her here with us."

That day Luther sent for Lena, and in a short time she arrived, happy to be near her niece and also happy to have a part in the life of the wonderful Dr. Luther.

As the days passed, Aunt Lena became aware of Katharine's loneliness. She readily saw what it was and saw also that Katharine was unreasonable. Dr. Luther and some of his colleagues were working on the translation of the Holy Scriptures, and they spent many hours on this work. Also, Luther preached almost every morning, taught in the university, and was pastor and counselor to the students of the university and to the parish. It was a mountainous task, and he was of necessity absorbed most of the time in the Lord's work. Katharine understood this, but at times she became impatient and unreasonable, wanting more of her husband for herself.

Aunt Lena felt sorry for her but said nothing. "She is young," she thought, "and has much to learn. The good doctor loves her, but he has so much important work that keeps him occupied most of the time. Katharine will have to be patient. In time she will see that she is wrong."

Katharine was grateful for Aunt Lena's help in the household.

One morning, arising at dawn as usual, Katharine felt an unfamiliar feeling of nausea. This persisted for several days, and she decided to visit the physician to see if there was anything seriously wrong.

A few hours later, when she left the physician's office, even the dirty streets of Wittenberg looked good to her. When she reached the parsonage, she went to Luther's study. Shy now, she stood in the doorway until Luther looked up and said, "What is it, Katharine?"

"I just returned from the physician," she said in a low voice, "and he tells me that I'm fine —"

"That's good," Luther interrupted. "I'm glad to hear it. I didn't think there was anything wrong with you."

Katharine was close to tears. With a great effort she swallowed and said, "He also told me that we're going to have a child."

Luther raised his eyes. There was still an absent-minded expression in his eyes, as though his thoughts were on the papers on his desk. "I'm glad, Katharine. I've been hoping and praying that God would bless us with a family."

Katharine stumbled out of the room and down the stairs,

blinded by tears. "The cow is going to have a calf too," she said. "I guess we're both in the same category as far as he's concerned!"

Upstairs Luther started after her, but she was gone. He walked back to his desk and bent his head. "Thank You, most gracious Father," he prayed, "for this wonderful gift You have bestowed on Katharine and me." He raised his head and with an effort resumed his work.

That afternoon Katharine was in the front yard visiting with her friend Eva Bugenhagen. "Oh, by the way," Katharine said in an offhand manner, "the doctor and I are going to have a baby. Probably in June."

"Oh, how wonderful, Katharine!" Eva said. "I'm so happy for you. Aren't you and the doctor thrilled?"

Katharine shrugged her shoulders. "Oh, not especially. It's just another mouth to feed."

Eva gasped. "How can you talk that way? What's wrong?"

Katharine's chin trembled, and she bit her lip. "Well, if the good doctor can be too busy to care, then so can I," she said.

Eva smiled. "So that's it! O Katharine, my dear, you really do misunderstand the good doctor. He's not too busy to care."

Katharine looked at her. "Do you really think so?"

"Of course I do. Already the doctor has been all over town telling everyone about it. He's so proud and happy."

Katharine smiled. "I guess I am foolish."

Eva patted her hand. "Wait until you see the doctor holding his child in his arms. Then you'll know what the rest of us already know."

Katharine changed the subject. "Eva, I'd like to have the women of our church have more Christian fellowship with one another. We can do a lot of good in the name of our Lord, ministering to the sick, feeding the poor —"

"O Katharine! It's a wonderful idea. I'll help in any way I can."

The women spent the rest of the afternoon discussing plans.

Spring progressed, and the first six days of June were hot and muggy. On the seventh day Katharine, walking alone in the garden, came upon Wolf and Luther working together. When she approached, Wolf bent his head lower to his work. Katharine was embarrassed. "I'm sorry if I interrupted you," she said. "I was just getting some exercise."

"Don't apologize, Katharine," Luther said. "You belong here. Doesn't she, Wolf?"

Wolf merely grunted and wielded the hoe furiously. He turned to Luther. "Why don't you and I go take a look at some of those wood-turning tools?" he asked.

Luther smiled. "A fine idea!" he said. "I need some practice on them."

The men walked toward the tool house, leaving Katharine alone. She stood in the warm sunshine and choked back the tears. When she saw Aunt Lena coming, she brushed the tears away.

"How are you feeling, dear?" Aunt Lena asked.

"I'm feeling a little —" Katharine started when a sudden pain stabbed at her. She turned pale. "O Aunt Lena, I think it's —"

Quickly Aunt Lena took her by the arm and helped her into the house.

Katharine lay in bed as Aunt Lena directed a servant to get the physician. Then she came to Katharine. "I'll go get Doctor Luther," she said.

Katharine grasped her hand. "No!" she cried. "Don't tell him!"

"Why not?"

Katharine bit her lip as a new pain clutched at her. "He'll find out soon enough," she said.

Aunt Lena stroked her forehead. "Katharine, my dear child," she said, "you're being so silly."

A few hours later Katharine opened her eyes and saw Luther standing over her. "O Katharine," he exclaimed, his eyes bright with happiness, "Kitty, my rib, you have brought forth a son."

Katharine smiled weakly. "Kitty! Kitty, my rib," she thought. "So! All she had to do was bring forth a son for the good doctor. Well!" She looked at her husband with new courage. "Dear Doctor, I love you. Tell me you love me."

He smiled at her over the tiny bundle in his arms. "I love you, Katharine. Oh, how I love you!"

"What shall we name the baby, Doctor?"

"He will be named after my dear father Hans."

"That's a good name."

Luther leaned over and kissed her tenderly. "I'm going to go get Chaplain Rohrer and Cranach and Dr. Bugenhagen and Jonas right away," he said.

"Why?" Katharine asked. "Is there something wrong with the baby?"

"No," Luther laughed, "of course not. I just want to have the little heathen baptized, that's all."

Outside the room Aunt Lena smiled. "Maybe now," she thought, "my dear niece will grow up a little."

It wasn't long before Katharine was up and taking care of her son. It soon became apparent to her that Aunt Lena regarded little Hans as her personal property and tried to take over the care of him whenever possible. Katharine decided to ignore it.

However, one day it became obvious that she was going to have to let Aunt Lena know how she felt. On that particular morning, just after Katharine had decided to bathe the baby, she discovered that Aunt Lena had already done it. When she started to take him out for some sunshine, Aunt Lena said, "Katharine, that baby has had enough sun for today. I took him out this morning."

Katharine's face was solemn as she turned to Aunt Lena. "When do you suppose that I will be able to care for my own child?" she asked.

Aunt Lena examined the tips of her shoes. "Well, Katharine, I think that you have enough to do as it is. I will care for Hans and relieve you of that burden anyway."

"Of course I have a lot to do, and I do it. All of it. Hans is a part of what I must do. My duty is to take care of the doctor's son, and it's no burden, as you call it." She smiled and added, "I gave birth to the doctor's son, and I shall care for him."

A light of understanding shone in Aunt Lena's eyes. "I see," she said, "but perhaps you and I can share in the care of Hans."

Katharine threw her arms around Aunt Lena. "Of course we will," she said. "Of course! O Aunt Lena, I'm so happy!"

Aunt Lena patted her shoulder. "Sure you are. A husband and a son all at the same time. I think perhaps my dear niece has grown up."

Katharine smiled. "I hope so."

Aunt Lena started down the hallway and then turned. "Did you tell me that the doctor called you 'Kitty, my rib'?"

"Yes," Katharine smiled, " 'Kitty, my rib' is what he called me."

Aunt Lena shook her head and went down the hall muttering to herself.

A few days later Wolf limped into the kitchen where Katherine was feeding little Hans. She noticed that he was standing behind her, not saying anything.

"Did you want something, Wolf?" she asked.

"No, Mistress Luther," Wolf answered. "I just came in to see the little one."

He stood silently and watched as Katharine fed the baby. When she rose, she turned to Wolf. "Would you like to hold him, Wolf?"

A look of awe crossed Wolf's face. "Would you let me?" he asked.

In answer Katharine put the baby in Wolf's arms. He sat for a long time, gently rocking the baby to and fro. Finally Katharine went to him. "I'm sorry, Wolf," she said, "but I must take him now. It's time for his nap." Wolf looked so disappointed that she hastily added, "You may come in later on in the afternoon and hold him if you'd like."

Wolf handed the baby to her. "Thank you, Mistress Luth —" He stopped and blushed a vivid red. "I mean, Mistress Katharine," he said and hastily left the house.

Katharine stood for long minutes staring after him. Finally she said, "Well! God be praised!" She snuggled her face into the baby's covers. "You are quite definitely an angel from heaven, my little son."

chapter nine

*T*HE DAYS WENT ON, and Katharine, now that she had, as Aunt Lena put it, grown up, found more happiness in parsonage life. She was a wife and a mother, and she realized now that she and her husband had another bond besides the one of love and parenthood. They were co-workers in the kingdom of God on earth. Now that she realized this and took happiness in it, her life was changed. She was happier than she had ever dreamed of being.

Luther's generous heart could not refuse anyone who came begging for help. Oftentimes, however, he found himself in the position of not having any money to give to those who asked for it. Yet he couldn't possibly conceive of turning anyone away empty-handed, not so long as he himself had anything. The Luthers at this period were nearly always deep in debt, and there were many times when Luther faced the predicament of not having a single coin to give. Then, like as not, he would pawn a silver vase or a goblet, or else he would give the beggar some other article of value, saying, "Here, take this. We have more. You can pawn it and get some money to tide you over."

Katharine knew this and disapproved in a quiet way that interfered not at all with his doing it. However, there was one Venetian glass goblet, a wedding gift, that she liked particularly. She was determined it should not be given away or pawned. "So many of our wedding gifts have been pawned already," she remarked to Aunt Lena, "and no doubt many more of them will go the same way in the years to come. The dear doctor is generous to a fault. I am determined that this lovely goblet shall not go too."

"What do you propose to do, Katharine? Hide it?" Aunt Lena asked.

"That's exactly what I shall do," she said with a smile. "I'll hide it, and I'll make sure that the dear doctor never finds the hiding place."

So the beautiful goblet was hidden that Luther might not pawn it or give it away.

Weeks passed, and Katharine felt sure that Luther would never miss the goblet. Finally she herself forgot about it. One summer day she told Luther that she wished there were some place for them to go for rest and relaxation. "We need to get away from the parsonage once in a while, Doctor," she said. Luther nodded and changed the subject.

A few days later Wolf and Luther came into the house and walked past Katharine without a word. They went into the study and closed the door behind them. Katharine wondered what they were up to.

Later in the day she approached Wolf and said in her most beguiling manner, "Wolf, are you and the doctor planning something special?"

Wolf grunted an unintelligible answer and went on with his work.

"Is it a big secret, Wolf?"

Wolf went on working and didn't answer. With a flip of her skirts, Katharine turned and walked away, leaving Wolf with a grin that spread from one side of his face to the other.

Katharine noticed, in the next few weeks, that Luther and Wolf often left the house in the morning, not returning until evening. One day she asked Luther what was going on.

"Why, my dear Katharine," Luther said with an air of innocence, "Wolf is just helping me learn how to operate the lathe tools."

"But why, dear Doctor?"

"Why? Who knows, I may need that skill one of these days. The ministers of religion are elected by their flocks, and their parishioners collect the minister's support among themselves."

"Those are the rules you yourself made, Doctor. Anyway, you are the university pastor and professor. Why are you worried?"

"I'm not worried, Katharine; but look at the miserable condition we ministers are in. They absolutely won't pay us. Here we have noblemen who in years gone by squandered thousands of florins upon designing knaves who plundered them, but now these same persons refuse to give one hundred to a worthy pastor. I really believe it's a good idea for a minister to have a trade to which he can turn in case he has to. I would rather make music my avocation, but I can't find a suitable teacher."

Katharine shrugged her shoulders. "As you wish, Doctor."

Several weeks later Luther and Wolf came to Katharine.

"My dear wife," Luther said, "will you please come with us? We have something to show you."

Puzzled, Katharine walked with them down the dusty

main street of Wittenberg. When they came to a little place near the Elster Gate on the Elbe River, Katharine caught her breath. "O dear Doctor!" she cried. "That summer house! Isn't it beautiful?"

Luther took her hand in his. "Do you like it, Katharine?"

Katharine nodded. "What a lovely place! Imagine a person having a little house like that right on the river. It would be so cool and inviting in the summer."

Wolf snickered, and Luther laughed out loud. "Katharine," he said, "that's our surprise. Wolf and I have been building it for you these past weeks."

Katharine looked at Luther, then at Wolf, and then at the summer house again.

"Why the tears?" Luther asked.

"Because I'm so happy. No other wife in the world is as fortunate as I am."

Several days later Luther remarked to Katharine, "I just received a letter from my old friend Agricola. He's in Eisleben and is getting married."

"I'm glad to hear it, Doctor," Katharine replied. "Will you go to the wedding?"

"No, but I shall send them a very, very nice gift."

"Doctor," Katharine said hurriedly, "we can't afford to buy something costly."

"I know that." He looked at his wife under arched brows. "Do you remember that very expensive, very lovely goblet that we received as a wedding gift?"

Katharine lowered her eyes. "Yes," she said in a very low voice.

"Well," Luther continued, "I remember that Agricola admired that especially. I recall that he held it and turned it this way and that and went on about its beauty at great length." He turned to Katharine. "I'll send him that for a wedding gift."

Katharine remained silent. Luther asked, "Where is the goblet?"

"Oh, somewhere in the parsonage, I'm sure." And hurriedly she left the room.

Later that evening Luther came to Katharine as she was feeding the baby. "Mrs. Luther," he said, "I just finished writing a long letter to my friend Agricola, congratulating him on his good fortune and wishing him and his bride a happy and fruitful union." He coughed and moved in front of her. "I also remarked that I would like to send him the goblet he so much admired, but since my wife has hidden it, I shall not be able to send it until I can find it."

Katharine blushed. "If you would only take some payment from the printers, we would have a little money with which to buy gifts when our friends get married."

"No, Katharine."

"But, dear Doctor," Katharine persisted, "there are nearly fifty printers in Wittenberg, and they are all making money from your writings. Why shouldn't you take payment from them?"

Luther shook his head. "No, Katharine. God will provide."

chapter ten

 ᒣHE WEEKS turned into summer, and
the Luther family continued in the Lord's work. Katharine
knew that Luther was working too hard, and she tried to
persuade him to take more rest, but except for the time when
he played with his son and talked quietly to Katharine before
they retired, he worked as hard as ever.

One morning Katharine awoke at dawn, and already the
day promised oppressive heat. Slowly she dressed and combed
her hair. She went immediately to the kitchen and started preparing breakfast. When the meal was nearly ready, she went
up to Luther's study. His huge desk sat forlornly in the middle
of the room. With a worried frown Katharine hurried to the
bedroom and found him in bed moaning.

"Dear Doctor!" she cried. "What's wrong? Are you ill?"

"O Katharine," Luther moaned, "I feel terrible. I don't
know what's wrong with me."

Katharine soaked a towel in a basin of water and wiped
his forehead and face. "Now, now, dear Doctor," she said, "it's
the heat. You'll be all right."

"The devil, in one form or another, will destroy Doctor
Luther," he said.

"You've been working too hard, dear Doctor. You're tired."

Katharine watched him with dismay. She hurried to the kitchen and prepared a tray. He refused the food and drink, and after a while she took the tray back to the kitchen. Aunt Lena looked at her with troubled eyes.

"What is it, Katharine? What's wrong with the doctor?"

Katharine sighed. "I don't know. I just don't know. I think it's exhaustion. The doctor works too hard." She threw a scarf over her head. "Aunt Lena, take care of things. I'm going to see Dr. Bugenhagen."

Katharine kicked up little clouds of dust as she hurried along the street. When she reached the parsonage and was seated across from Dr. Bugenhagen, she let out a deep sigh.

"Pastor," she began, "I don't know what's wrong with my husband. He won't eat or drink. He has a fever, and he cries like a baby."

Dr. Bugenhagen folded his hands and said, "Why didn't you go to Physician Schurf, Katharine?"

She looked into his eyes. "Because Dr. Luther said that the devil is trying to destroy him."

Dr. Bugenhagen rose and paced. "Nonsense!" he said.

"Nonsense? What do you mean?"

"Luther didn't mean that. You misunderstood him. His body is taking revenge now for all the sins committed against it. In the convent he abused himself terribly, and ever since has worked too hard and had too little recreation. That's all there is to it, and Luther knows it. When he says that the devil is trying to destroy him, he means that the devil, in the form of physical exhaustion, is keeping him from the Lord's work."

Katharine nodded. "You're his father-confessor. Will you come and talk to him?"

"Of course I will. Let's go."

Dr. Bugenhagen spent most of the early morning hours talking to Luther. Katharine worked in the garden and tended to the baby, but she worked listlessly. Finally Dr. Bugenhagen came out of Luther's bedroom.

"Come, Katharine," he said, "you can help me. I've reminded Brother Martin that the Elector's marshal has invited us to breakfast. You try to convince him that he should go."

"Are you sure it will be all right for him to go?"

"Of course it will. It will be relaxation, and that's what he needs."

Luther was finally persuaded to go to the breakfast.

Katharine watched the men leave the house. "I hope I did right," she thought. "I hope it was right for me to persuade him to go."

The morning dragged for Katharine. She was anxious for Luther to return. After a silent noonday meal she rocked the baby to sleep and then waited for Luther. By midafternoon she was really worried and hurried out to Wolf. He watched her coming toward him, and there was a question in his eyes.

"What is it, Mistress Luther?" he asked. "Is anything wrong with the doctor?"

Katharine held out her hands to him. "O Wolf, I'm terribly worried. The doctor went to the breakfast this morning and hasn't returned yet. Do you suppose —"

Wolf interrupted her. "I'll go down to Dr. Bugenhagen's," he said.

Katharine watched him as he painfully hobbled down the street. In a short time he returned, his face ashen. He spoke calmly. "The doctor left after the breakfast this morning, Mistress Luther," he said, "and the others noticed that he was very quiet and ate little. He left as soon as it was over, and Dr. Bugenhagen said he assumed that the doctor had gone home."

"No one knows where he is, then?" Katharine asked.

Wolf shook his head.

"O Wolf, what are we going to do?"

Wolf again shook his head. Silently he walked away from her.

Katharine told Aunt Lena what had happened.

"Nothing's happened to the doctor," Aunt Lena said. "So stop worrying."

"How do you know nothing's happened to him?"

"I just know, that's all. Now tend to your child." Aunt Lena spoke with a brave smile, but as Katharine left the room, her eyes followed her, and a frown erased the smile.

In the late afternoon, just at suppertime, Luther came home. Katharine flung herself into his arms. "O Doctor," she cried, "where have you been? I've been so worried!"

Luther held her close. "I decided to have a talk with Justus Jonas. He's a dear friend, and I feel better now."

Katharine brushed away a tear. "Well, just so you really do feel better," she said.

At the supper table Luther didn't feel like eating. Katharine pleaded, "Please, dear Doctor, eat. You need your strength."

He sighed and pushed his plate away. "I'm sorry, Katharine; I can't force it down my throat." Then, starting for the door, he said, "I invited Justus Jonas over for this evening, so I think I'll lie down until he comes."

When Justus arrived, he found the parsonage a site of confusion. Katharine looked at him with fright in her eyes.

"The doctor's sick, Justus," she said, "very sick. I don't know what to do."

Justus put an arm around her. "Calm down, Katharine. What happened?"

"He didn't eat any supper. He went to bed saying he

was going to lie down until you came. A few minutes ago I went in and found him crying."

Justus followed Katharine into the bedroom. Luther told him of feeling dizzy and faint and of hearing great rushing, whirring noises in his head. Katharine stood at his side, biting the knuckles of her hand. Justus stood at the foot of the bed, looking at his friend.

"Water!" Luther cried. "Give me water!"

Justus hurried to the basin and brought a cup of water. He hesitated for a second and then threw the water into Luther's face. "Maybe that will bring him out of it," he said.

Instead, Luther's body stiffened, and his eyes rolled upward. Katharine felt his forehead. "He's getting cold," she said. In panic, she ran out of the house. She held up her skirts and ran down the dusty road in the semidarkness until she reached the home of Augustus Schurf, the family physician. She panted out in a few words what had happened. Dr. Schurf grabbed his bag and came to the door.

"You go ahead," Katharine said. "I'll be right behind you."

Dr. Schurf nodded and started running toward the parsonage. When Katharine finally reached Luther's bedroom, the doctor had him wrapped in heated cloths. Aunt Lena and Justus were running back and forth with the cloths.

Katharine knelt beside her husband. He was whispering. "Dear Father, into Thy hands I commend my spirit."

Katharine looked at Dr. Schurf. "He thinks he's dying."

Dr. Schurf looked at her and didn't answer the question in her eyes.

Luther turned his head. "Don't cry, Katharine. Don't be afraid. Don't lose faith. God will take care of you. He is everywhere with you." Then, as Katharine buried her face in the palm of his hand, he said, "Will you bring Hans to me?"

76

Immediately Katharine rose and ran to the baby's room. She brought him to Luther, and he kissed his son and said, "I commend you both to the Lord."

Aunt Lena took Hans away, and Katharine again knelt at Luther's side. A ghostly hush had fallen over the room. Dr. Schurf and Justus Jonas stood at the foot of the bed, not knowing what to do, feeling that nothing would do any good. Aunt Lena stood near the doorway, using the corner of her apron for a handkerchief.

Katharine stayed on her knees. Presently, in a low voice, she said, "Dear Doctor, I don't want you to die. I need you, and your son needs you, and many Christian people need your strength and your guidance. I hope that God will spare your life." She stopped, then added, "However, God's will be done. The Lord giveth, and the Lord taketh away. Blessed be the name of the Lord. Amen."

Justus looked at the slim figure kneeling at the bedside and felt new hope. "Let's try to rub his arms and legs," he said.

As they rubbed, they prayed for his life. After long, torturous hours he revived. Katharine fed him some chicken broth, and he slept. She turned to Dr. Schurf. Tears came to her eyes, and she threw herself at the physician's feet. "Thank you," she sobbed, "thank you!"

Dr. Schurf helped her to her feet. "You're exhausted, Katharine," he said. "You must sleep now while the doctor sleeps."

Katharine squeezed his hand. "First," she said, "let's thank God for this miracle." She led them in prayer. Then they all said together, "Amen," and silently left the room.

Katharine looked down at her husband's sleeping face. She made the sign of the cross. "God be praised!" she whispered.

Physically Luther was well, but mentally he was despondent. He fell into a state of lethargy, and nothing seemed able to bring him out of it. He sat and stared into space and was sad. Katharine tried everything she could think of to bring him out of it, but nothing worked.

Dr. Bugenhagen came over daily to talk to him and try to cheer him. "Something's got to happen to bring him out of this state of mind," he told Katharine. "There's no fight left in the good doctor."

Katharine didn't answer. She stared at the closed study door with a thoughtful expression.

That evening she went to her room and dressed in her mourning clothes. As a final touch she also put on a heavy black veil that covered her face. She went slowly up the stairs and entered Luther's study. He was sitting at his desk, his hands idle, his eyes staring vacantly into space. When he saw his wife, his mouth dropped open. "Katharine! What's the matter? Why are you dressed in mourning?"

Katharine turned a sad face toward her husband. "Oh," she said, "it's terrible, terrible!"

"What is?"

"God is dead," she answered, shaking her head.

"God is dead?" Luther thundered. "What in heaven's name are you talking about?"

"Are you not Doctor Luther?" Katharine asked. "Are you not my pastor as well as my husband?"

He nodded dumbly.

"Then, judging by your actions these past few weeks, I can see that God is dead. If He weren't, you would use your great faith in Him to help you out of this lethargy."

Luther stared at her for a long time. Then he said, "You're right, Katharine." He bowed his head and added, "I'm ashamed of myself."

Katharine rushed to him. "Don't be ashamed, dear Doctor. It happens to all of us. I just wanted to help you see what you're doing."

Luther put his arms around her. "You helped, Katharine; you helped a great deal. Now if you will please change your clothes and leave me alone, I shall get busy."

"You're going to start working this very minute?"

"Yes, this very minute."

 $\mathcal{L}$UTHER had come out of his sickness and his lethargy, and Katharine rejoiced to see him again working and feeling well.

Then the plague struck Wittenberg. The citizens in their terror forgot even human decency. Their fear made them desert their dying, and bodies lay heaped grotesquely on the streets.

The Elector commanded the students and professors to go to Jena until the plague was over. Luther stormed into the Elector's office when he heard this. "I shall not go," he said. "I dare not go!"

The Elector looked at him and decided not to try to convince him to leave. Luther hurried back to the parsonage, where Katharine met him at the door. "We've got to hurry," she said.

"Hurry? For what?"

"Why, to get out of here, of course."

Without answering Luther walked to his study, and Katharine followed. Dr. Bugenhagen and Chaplain Rohrer were waiting for him.

"Doctor Luther," Rohrer began, "what do you plan to do?"

"I shall remain here and help in any way that I can," Luther replied.

Katharine gasped. "Dear Doctor, do you know what you're saying?"

"Yes, of course I do. I shall remain. I dare not do otherwise."

Chaplain Rohrer walked over to Luther. "I'll stay also and help," he said and left the room.

Dr. Bugenhagen rose and sighed. "I, too, Brother Martin, will do all I can." And he also left.

Katharine stood as though rooted. "I don't understand you," she said in a tight voice.

"I'm sorry, Katharine."

"Sorry? What about Hans, your dear son, and me, your wife? When we die of the plague, I suppose you'll say you're sorry?"

Luther waited until the sound of her words had died, then he turned to her. "Katharine, I'm a pastor. I can't leave. 'The good shepherd giveth his life for his sheep; but he that is an hireling seeth the wolf coming and leaveth the sheep and fleeth.'"

The ensuing silence was long. Katharine's eyes stayed glued to her husband. Finally she spoke, "I'm sorry, dear Doctor. We'll stay. When you're ready for me to work, tell me what I'm to do."

"Are you sure, Katharine?"

"I'm your wife. I dare not leave."

The days that followed were like a nightmare. Katharine gave instructions to Aunt Lena. "Keep Hans in your bedroom, Aunt Lena. Don't let him out. Bring his meals up to his room, and stay with him."

Aunt Lena nodded. "I don't think that you should be

doing this in your condition. Your second child is well on the way. I was hoping I could help you and the doctor."

Katharine grabbed her shoulders. "If you save the doctor's son from the plague —" she began, but tears choked back any more words.

"I understand, Katharine," Aunt Lena said. "I'll do as you say."

For the first few days Luther and Katharine left the parsonage early in the morning and went their separate ways. They went from house to house, helping wherever they were needed. They returned at night, very late, to catch a few hours' sleep before dawn. Katharine's face was pale and drawn, and she was very tired.

"Doctor," she said one night as they were getting ready for bed, "are you feeling all right?"

Luther held her in his arms. "Of course I am," he said. "Dear Katharine, you're not to worry about me. You have enough to do and think about."

Katharine smiled and kissed him good night. In a few minutes they were asleep.

At dawn they rose, and after a hearty breakfast, eaten in haste, Katharine started to leave the house. Dr. Schurf and his family met her at the door. "May we stay here?" he asked. "There's no place for us to go, and we're all sick with the pl—" and he fell at Katharine's feet.

She helped Luther carry him into the house and put him to bed. She put him in Luther's bed and his wife in hers and stayed home to care for them.

Later in the day others came to the parsonage and, after all the beds were filled, she laid mats on the floor. Wolf helped her nurse the sick, and he carried the dead out to make room for others. Every night Katharine visited Hans and Aunt Lena upstairs in the little bedroom.

"He's getting so pale and thin, Aunt Lena," Katharine cried one night at the sight of her son.

"So are you, Katharine," Aunt Lena said in a tired voice. "I think you should stay here with Hans and let me work out there."

Katharine shook her head. "No, Aunt Lena. This is something that I must do. I'll be all right."

"But your unborn child!" Aunt Lena pleaded. "It will be here in a few months."

Katharine started for the door. "Not until December," she said. "I have nearly four months. The plague will be gone by then."

Aunt Lena sighed. "You shouldn't be doing this, Katharine. You shouldn't be doing it."

"On the contrary," Katharine smiled, "I'm Doctor Martin Luther's wife. I must be doing it."

The days and weeks seemed long, and Katharine worked to the point of exhaustion every day. Many nights she would fall into a heavy sleep only to be awakened by someone sobbing or crying out in pain.

Chaplain Rohrer brought his young wife to the parsonage. "I'm sorry, Katharine," he said, "to burden you any more, but she's sick with the plague, and our child is due any day."

Katharine's heart ached for him. She made sure that his wife was comfortable and then turned to him, "I'll take good care of her. She'll be all right."

He looked down at his wife. "Thank you, Katharine. I'll leave now. There's much to be done. She's in God's hands now."

That evening Luther returned to the parsonage, and Katharine took him by the hand and silently led him to

Mrs. Rohrer's side. He looked down at the sleeping face and whispered, "She's so young and so beautiful, isn't she, Katharine?"

Katharine nodded, and tears filled her eyes. "Their baby is due in a short while," she said.

Luther continued to look at the young woman, and Katharine said, "O Doctor, he apologized when he brought her here!"

Luther nodded. Then he put his arms around her and held her close. "Katharine, my beloved wife. God has spared me so far."

Katharine clung to him. "God be praised!" she said.

The days wore on, and still the plague raged. The air was beginning to chill, and one night Luther said to Katharine, "Soon it will be winter, and the plague will go."

Katharine only nodded and kept on with her work. She was numb with weariness, and her increasing size made it difficult for her to care for the patients. Luther put his arm around her and gently led her into the kitchen. On the floor was a pallet. "Lie down, Katharine," he said, "and sleep. Sleep until dawn."

Katharine protested. "But, Doctor, what if one of the patients should wake and need me? I couldn't hear them here in the kitchen."

"Wolf and I will watch tonight. They're all quiet, and I want you to sleep. Please, Katharine."

Gratefully she lay down and in a few minutes was sound asleep. In the morning she awoke feeling more refreshed than she had for weeks. As she was eating breakfast, Wolf came into the kitchen. "You'd best go to the doctor," he said.

Katharine looked at him in alarm. "Wolf," she asked, "what is it?"

Wolf choked back tears. "He needs you," he said and went outside.

Katharine hurried to Luther's study. He sat hunched forward, his great body shaking and tears streaming down his face. When Katharine went to him, he put his arms around her and held her close. "Katharine," he sobbed, "Chaplain Rohrer's beautiful young wife and their unborn child are dead."

The impact of what he had said left Katharine speechless. Presently she, too, cried. When they had controlled their tears, Luther said, "I haven't much heart to continue."

Katharine nodded. "I know," she said.

When Dr. Bugenhagen came to the study, he found Luther and Katharine listless and sad. "You can't give up now," he pleaded.

Luther looked at him. "She was so young and beautiful, and they had looked forward to the birth of their first child. This is a great blow to us."

Dr. Bugenhagen turned to Katharine. "I know all this, but we can't give up. She wouldn't have wanted us to."

Tears came to Katharine's eyes. "We're not giving up," she said in a small voice. "It's just that we've lost heart."

Dr. Bugenhagen moved uneasily. "Doctor Schurf, thank God, is well again."

Katharine sighed. "God be praised for that! His dear wife is dead though." She turned to Luther. "It's almost more than I can bear, dear Doctor."

He patted her hand. "God never sends us more than we can bear, dear wife," he said gently. "You know that."

She squeezed his hand in answer and left the room.

chapter twelve

═══════════

 $\mathcal{T}$HE WINTER STORMS began, and the
plague seemed to be leaving. There were fewer deaths, and no
new cases were appearing. On the tenth of December, right
after the noon meal, Katharine laboriously climbed the stairs
to Hans's room. She found him and Aunt Lena playing a
game. She held her son in her arms for a long while, then
released him. "He's so thin and pale, Aunt Lena," she said.

Aunt Lena's eyes caressed the boy. "He's had a lot of
trouble with his teeth, poor lamb. But he's all right now.
What about you?"

Katharine smiled. "I'm going to bed. I think that very
soon Hans will have a brother or sister."

Aunt Lena rushed to her. "Then go. Get in bed. I'll
take care of everything and I'll see that Dr. Schurf is on hand."

Katharine smiled her thanks and left the room.

That afternoon Dr. Schurf came out of Katharine's room
and handed a soft, tiny bundle to Luther. "Your daughter,"
he said.

Luther peeked at the tiny red face. "She's so little, so terribly little. Is she healthy?"

Dr. Schurf laughed. "Of course she's healthy. She's just tiny."

Luther handed the baby to Aunt Lena and went to Katharine and knelt at her side. She opened her eyes and turned toward him with a faint smile. "God be praised!" she said.

Luther took one of her hands and pressed it to his lips. "God be praised!" he repeated. "We have one more instead of one less. He has blessed us greatly."

Katharine closed her eyes. "God is good to us, dear Doctor, so good to us. He is everywhere with us." Then she fell asleep.

The severe winter raged on, and slowly Wittenberg returned to normal. The fugitive students and professors returned, the sick were up and about, and the dead had been buried. That Christmas there was much sadness in the town. So many had lost loved ones, and everyone grieved the loss of friends.

The Luthers gathered around their Christmas tree. Baby Elizabeth slept in her cradle, and Hans danced with joy at the gifts he received. Katharine and Luther were solemn, thinking of Dr. Schurf's wife and Chaplain Rohrer's wife and child. Luther read the Christmas story from Luke with more than his usual fervor.

Then the winter storms abated, and before long spring came. Katharine looked at the muddy streets. "Sometimes," she remarked, "I think that I like the winter best. Then at least the roads are white and clean."

Life in the parsonage continued as before. Many students lived with the Luthers and ate their meals with them. At each evening meal, after devotions and prayers, the students sat at the long table and listened eagerly to Luther. Some took notes on all that he said. Their friends dropped in occasionally for talk and a glass of beer.

Then summer came, and with the stifling heat they slowed their pace. One very hot afternoon in July Katharine went to Luther's study and found his great head bent over his desk. "Doctor," she said, "it's very warm today. Could we take the children to the summer house? Perhaps it's cool down there."

"Poor Katharine," Luther replied, "you have so little rest and relaxation; then you have to come begging for what you do get." He rose and took her hands in his. "Get Hans and baby Elizabeth ready, and we'll go down for a few hours."

In a short time Hans was toddling down the street beside Aunt Lena with Luther and Katharine behind them. Katharine held baby Elizabeth in her arms. When they reached the summer house, Hans played in the grassy shade; Aunt Lena sewed as she kept an eye on him. Luther drew a soft, haunting melody from his lute, and Katharine gently rocked her daughter. It was cool and quiet, and the Luther family basked in a rare moment of peace and tranquillity. The summer house was a cool haven of refuge, and Katharine was thankful for it. It nestled among the trees, and the dark-green grass gave it an appearance of quiet serenity. Behind it the rushing waters of the Elbe River seemed to Katharine to be calling to her to come, to enjoy the peacefulness it offered. Whenever she went near it, hurrying to market or to visit a parishioner, she looked at it longingly. "It's such a beautiful place," she often thought. "Why can't we enjoy it more often?" Now Katharine looked at her daughter's sleeping face. "Doctor," she said softly, "do you think baby Elizabeth is well?"

Luther laughed. "How could I think otherwise? Look at the roses blooming in her cheeks."

Katharine smiled, eager to believe that Luther was right.

She couldn't quite stifle, however, a vague feeling of apprehension.

"Mother! Mother! Look!" Hans scrambled to his feet and started to run down the road. They all looked up to see Wolf limping toward them. In his hands he carried a small wooden horse. When Hans reached him, Wolf picked him up and carried him and the wooden horse to the summer house.

"What is that wooden thing?" Luther asked.

"It's not a thing, doctor," Wolf answered haughtily; "it's a toy horse for Hans to play with. I made it this morning." He handed the toy to Hans, and the boy jumped up and down with delight. Wolf seated himself on the grass to play with the boy, and Luther resumed playing the lute.

Katharine finally broke the silence. "Doctor, why don't you read to us from Scripture? It's been a long time since we've all been together like this."

Luther took his Bible from his pocket and opened it at random. "I'll read the story of Abraham's sacrifice," he said. "And it came to pass after these things, that God did tempt Abraham —"

Katharine listened to the story of Abraham being called upon by God to give up his son. Several times she looked at Hans playing with his new toy, and then her eyes searched her daughter's face. When Luther had finished reading, she said, "I can't believe that God would ask a child of His to make a sacrifice like that."

"But He did," Luther replied. "It was a testing of Abraham's faith."

Katharine smiled. "He didn't have to go through with it though."

"The point is, he was willing to. God knew what was in Abraham's heart. Many times things happen to us in our lives, and God uses them to test our faith."

Katharine shook her head. She drew her arms a little

89

tighter around the baby. "I'm sure I would fail the test," she said. "I wouldn't be able to do it."

Luther said nothing, but his eyes remained on his wife in a thoughtful gaze.

A few weeks later, on the third of August, Katharine was sitting in the shade of the big pear tree in front of the parsonage when Luther came out.

"Doctor," she cried, "I really do believe that baby Elizabeth is ill."

Luther came to her and held the baby in his arms for a few minutes. "Katharine," he said, "Elizabeth is fine. You worry too much." He put the baby in her arms. "I wish you wouldn't worry so needlessly. It shows a lack of faith." He walked over to the garden and returned with a rose. He held the flower to the baby's face. "See? Her cheeks are as red and beautiful as this rose. And her eyes are as bright and shining as the stars in the heavens."

Luther seemed satisfied that Elizabeth was well, but Katharine wasn't; so, that evening she sent Wolf for the physician. When Dr. Schurf came, he spent a long time examining the baby. Then he looked into Katharine's questioning eyes. There were no words spoken, but Katharine knew what his silence meant. She gasped and ran from the room. Luther took her in his arms and kissed the top of her head.

When Dr. Schurf came into the room, Luther looked at him. "Dr. Schurf," he said in a weak voice, "she can't be that ill. Why, she looked so healthy. There were —" tears rushed to his eyes, "there were roses in her cheeks," he finished.

Dr. Schurf hung his head. "I'm so sorry," he said.

Katharine and Luther went into the baby's room and knelt at her bedside. They were silent, watching the child's breathing. Then Katharine put her face into her hands and cried, "O dear Father, let this cup pass from us. It is so bitter that I cannot drink it!"

The baby died that night. The next morning, overcome with grief, Katharine stayed in bed.

Wolf made a wooden cross, and Luther wrote on it: "Here sleeps Elizabeth, Martin Luther's little daughter." She was buried next to the parsonage.

Gradually Luther emerged from the blackness of his grief. Katharine, however, took no interest in anything. Aunt Lena bore her grief with dignity, but Katharine, for weeks to come, stayed in bed. When she did get up for brief periods of time, she worked with an apathy and clung to Hans with an intensity that frightened him.

Then one day, a few months after Elizabeth's death, Luther called the physician to the parsonage. "Katharine is really ill," Luther told him. "I'm worried about her. Her grief for our baby is great, I know, but now I think that something else is wrong."

Dr. Schurf went to Katharine, and when he again faced Luther, his face was wreathed in smiles. "She's going to have a baby," he said.

Luther went in to his wife and held her in his arms.

"A new life is beginning," he said. "Does this make you happy again?"

Katharine clung to him. "Dear Doctor," she whispered, "of course it makes me happy. I'm sorry that I have grieved for so long over baby Elizabeth."

"You were weak and tired, dear wife, that's all."

Katharine lay back on her pillow. "I've been thinking," she said thoughtfully, "about what you said before baby Elizabeth died. About God testing Abraham."

Luther nodded.

"God tested me too, and I failed, didn't I?"

91

Luther took her hand in his. "How can you say that? God used this to bring about something good in your life. All things work together for good to them who love God. Perhaps this has worked for good."

Katharine smiled. "It has, dear Doctor; indeed it has." She got out of bed then and resumed her duties. She no longer hugged Hans with such intensity, and he again bubbled over with laughter.

"This makes a difference, doesn't it, Katharine?" Luther asked.

"No child can ever replace baby Elizabeth," Katharine replied, "but I will be so happy to have another daughter in my arms."

"Wait! Wait!" Luther cried. "Maybe you'll have a son."

Katharine smiled. "I'll have a daughter," she said firmly.

Several weeks later Katharine walked into Luther's study. He sat at his desk in a state of dejection, his head slumped on his chest. His hands were idle at his sides. She went to him and placed her hands on his shoulders. "What's the matter, dear Doctor?" she asked. "You have been like this for days now. What is it that's troubling you?"

Slowly he raised his head. "Katharine, I don't know what's wrong. The devil is plaguing me again."

Katharine removed her hand with an impatient gesture. "It is not the devil," she said sharply. "We can't blame him for everything. It's something else."

Luther's smile was sad. "You don't hold much with my beliefs about the devil, do you?"

"No, I don't. Not for everything that goes wrong."

"Then I can't tell you what is wrong with me. All I know is that I have fallen into a terrible and frightening state of lethargy and that I can't write or read or do anything without having this awful buzzing and ringing start in my ears. My head becomes filled with all sorts of whizzing, buzzing, thundering noises, and if I did not leave off reading on the instant, I should faint away. For the last few days I have not even looked at a letter."

"You don't eat properly, you don't sleep properly, you don't —"

Luther interrupted her. "Don't start talking with the tongue of a wife. I know I don't do any of those things, because I can't — it's all a part of this lethargy. I can't help it."

Katharine sighed and walked toward the door. "I have a lot of work to do," she announced, holding her head high. "I can't afford to go into a state of lethargy. There is much that I must accomplish before I go to bed tonight."

"Perhaps it's just that I'm an old man."

Katharine stopped as though a huge hand had detained her. Instantly she was at his side, her arms around his shoulders. "Forgive me for being so impatient," she said. "I'm sorry. You're not an old man. You have so much to offer the world that I will never have. It's just that I worry about you. I love you and don't want to lose you."

"Katharine, God has greatly blessed me by giving me such a faithful wife as you."

She smiled and ran a hand over the top of his head. "I long ago wondered, dear Doctor, what God's will for me was. If I can bring even a little love and comfort to a man such as you, I am happy."

chapter thirteen

ON THE FOURTH of May, 1530, Magdalene was born.

"Little Lena," Luther said as he held her in his arms. "Katharine, you were right. A beautiful daughter."

Katharine smiled happily and drifted into an untroubled sleep. In a few days she was up, caring for her children and assuming her parsonage duties.

Shortly after Lena's birth Luther announced that he was going to Coburg. "I will probably be gone for some time," he told Katharine.

"How long?"

"Several months." When he saw her look of dismay, he hastily added, "Now, Katharine, maybe I'm wrong." He shrugged his shoulders. "I just don't know how long I'll have to be away."

Tight-lipped, Katharine asked, "Why are you going? What is it this time?"

"The Diet of Augsburg."

Katharine looked at him in surprise. "And you're going to Coburg?"

Luther pulled at his lower lip. "The imperial interdict forbids my attendance at the Diet, but the Protestants want me at Coburg."

"Why?"

Impatient now, Luther replied, "Coburg is very near to Augsburg, Katharine. They can come to me for advice."

Katharine sewed furiously. "I know that you'll tell me all about your duties to the Protestants and that you're here to do the Lord's work, dear Doctor, but you've been ill. Must you go?"

Luther's eyes flashed. "Germany is menaced from without by the threat of war and from within as to its liberty of faith." He paced before her. "Katharine, my main trouble lately has been an awful state of lethargy, an unwillingness to work. This double threat to Germany is going to help me, not hurt me."

Katharine continued her sewing. "I hope you're right, dear Doctor."

Luther had been in Coburg for several weeks.

"Katharine," Aunt Lena snapped one day, "if you don't stop walking around sighing all the time, I'll go mad."

"I'm sorry, Aunt Lena," Katharine answered. "It's just that the days seem endless. The same things happen at the same time every day. Nothing different or exciting or unexpected ever happens."

Aunt Lena smiled. "You miss the doctor."

"It's different around here when the doctor's not home," Katharine agreed.

That afternoon a messenger brought a letter for Katharine. She sat in Luther's study near the window and read it with tears in her eyes. Aunt Lena entered the study. When she saw Katharine's tears, she ran to her. "Bad news, Katharine? Bad news from the doctor?"

"No, Aunt Lena, not bad news. It's just that I'm so happy to hear from him."

Her aunt shrugged her shoulders. "So you cry."

Katharine nodded. "Listen, Aunt Lena, to what he says here." She read aloud, her face wreathed in smiles. "Katharine, you have a husband who loves you. Many an empress is not so well off. Thanks be unto God." Katharine looked up into her aunt's face. "Aren't they beautiful words, Aunt Lena?"

Aunt Lena sniffed and started for the door. "I guess so," she said in a husky voice. "Never having had a husband, I wouldn't know." Just as she reached the door, she heard Katharine gasp. She wheeled around. "What is it, Katharine, another bunch of beautiful words?"

"The dear doctor says that there are some Spaniards at the Diet of Augsburg who seriously believe that Dr. Luther and I are destined to produce Antichrist."

In the silence that followed the women looked into each other's eyes. Aunt Lena spoke loudly. "Katharine! Surely that's the most terrible nonsense I've heard in a long time."

"Of course it's nonsense, but it's vicious too. I don't like for the doctor to be bothered by things like that."

"Hah!" Aunt Lena snorted, "I'll wager he's not the least bit upset. He'll be able to dismiss the rumor just like that." She tried unsuccessfully to snap her fingers and left the room.

A few days later Katharine received news of the death of Luther's father. She went into Luther's study and sat at the great oaken desk trying to sort her thoughts. "There must be something that I can do for him," she thought. Her heart ached to be able to lay a comforting hand on his or to speak softly, as a wife can, and ease the sorrow she knew lay heavily on his heart. Finally a light appeared in her eyes, and she jumped from the desk. She returned with a small portrait of little Lena. With a smile she prepared it for the messenger to take the next morning to Luther. Later she told Aunt Lena, "I'm sending that very good little portrait of Lena to the doctor. I think it will help to ease the loss of his dear father."

Aunt Lena grinned. "Just the mention of that little one would make him feel better."

In the meantime Katharine waited for Luther's return to Wittenberg. She kept herself busy visiting with some of the women of the church. She and Eva Bugenhagen and a few others met once a week. They had a short devotional period and then discussed ways and means of furthering their missionary efforts. The women comforted the sick, contributed food and clothing to the poor, and encouraged all to attend the Lutheran services. Katharine enjoyed this work, and slowly the group was growing. It was unofficial, but they had no difficulty getting the women to join them in their work. This, plus what she was able to do for others in the parsonage, helped to give her a feeling that she was of real assistance to Luther. The activity also eased the loneliness she felt when he was away. When he at last returned from Coburg, she threw herself into his arms. "O dear Doctor," she said, "I missed you so much! I wish you never had to leave me."

Luther kissed her and held her tightly. "It's good to be home, dear wife," he said. "It's good to be home." Then the parsonage routine returned to normal.

Shortly after Hans's fifth birthday, Luther said to Katharine, "I believe the boy needs tutoring."

"He's so young, dear Doctor," Katharine protested. "Couldn't we wait another year?"

Luther shook his head. "He's so spoiled and so much

97

trouble all the time, I think it would be best for him to spend several hours a day trying to learn something. If he doesn't learn anything, it will at least keep him out of trouble."

Katharine's face showed her displeasure. "I wish you'd stop saying that Hans is such a bad boy."

"He is a bad, disobedient boy," Luther insisted.

"He's little more than a baby."

"Katharine, you spoil that boy."

"I do not spoil him any more than you spoil little Lena."

Luther grinned. "If little Lena were like Hans, I should not spoil her; but her sweet disposition cannot be spoiled." Luther saw that his wife was close to tears. Quickly, he took her in his arms. "My dear wife, we are arguing over our children. I'm sorry."

"I'm sorry too, dear Doctor."

The Luthers made up after the quarrel, but it was indeed true that little Hans was a troublesome, disobedient child. Perhaps Katharine had spoiled him somewhat, but after their discussion she tried to discipline him. The boy improved and was a delight to his parents. It was to Hans that Luther wrote the following:

Grace and peace in Christ, my dear little son:

I am glad to hear that you are studying well and saying your prayers faithfully. Continue to do so, Sonny, and when I come home, I will bring you a fine gift.

I know a lovely, pleasant park where there are many children. They wear golden jackets and gather nice apples under the trees, and pears and cherries and purple and yellow plums. They sing, skip, and are merry; they also have pretty little ponies with golden bridles and silver saddles. Then I asked the owner of the park who the children were.

He replied, "These are the children who like to pray and learn, who are pious children."

I said to him, "Dear friend, I also have a son, whose name is little Hans Luther; couldn't he also come here and eat these nice apples and pears and ride these fine ponies and play with the other children?"

The man replied, "If he likes to pray and studies hard and is a good boy, he may come into the park too — Phil and Justy too. And when they all come, they shall also have fifes, drums, lutes, and all sorts of musical instruments; and dance, too, and shoot little crossbows."

In the park he also showed me a beautiful lawn all prepared for dancing, with golden fifes and drums and crossbows hung up all around. But it was still early, and the children had not yet breakfasted, and I just couldn't wait till the dancing started. Therefore I said to the man, "Dear sir, I will go as fast as I can and write all about this to my dear little son Hans and tell him to be a good boy, to pray faithfully and study well, that he may come to this park too. But he has an Aunt Lena he must bring along."

The man answered, "Yes, go ahead and write him that it shall be so."

Therefore, dear Hans, study and pray well, and tell Phil and Justy to say their prayers and study too; then you may all come into the beautiful park. Be commended to the care of Almighty God. Greet Aunt Lena, and give her a kiss for me. The year 1530.

Your loving father,

Martin Luther

Hans was overjoyed at receiving the letter and had his mother read it to him over and over.

Katharine was very happy. Luther, though absorbed in his work most of the time, always managed some time of the day for his family. Hans and little Lena adored their father, and his love kept Katharine going through the long days. Every night she thanked God for a Christian husband and father. Her busy days were made joyful and easy by one loving glance from her husband.

One night at the evening meal when, as usual, the Luther table was filled with platters of crisp fried fish, chicken, fruits, and vegetables — for their guests and many boarders were hearty eaters — Luther spoke the prayer after all had eaten, leaned back, and said, "Well, what's new? What shall we talk about?"

In the ensuing chatter Katharine looked across the table. The eager, shining faces of the young students as they looked toward Luther filled her with happiness. "How they hang on his every word!" she thought. "How they need his guidance!"

Luther spoke to her. "Katharine, isn't it true that we should all read and hear with correct attention the Word of God, most especially the Psalms?"

Katharine looked at her husband and then down the table at the students. "I already listen sufficiently," she answered primly, "and I read portions of Scripture every day so that I am able to recite a great number of passages from it."

Luther sighed. "And so we start to take the Word of God too lightly. It's a sign of ill promise. One of these days some new books will be started in competition, and Holy Scripture will be slighted, despised, jerked into a corner, thrown, as they say, under the table." He paused and looked again at his wife.

As he talked, Katharine rose and beckoned to the children. "Come," she whispered to them, "it's time for bed." After she had undressed the children and spent her usual few minutes telling them about the wonders of God and His precious Son, she tucked them into bed and called Luther. He came into the room and kissed them. Then he and Katharine knelt beside their beds for prayers. When he had finished, they made the sign of the cross and rose to leave the room.

Katharine stopped him at the door. "They are wonderful, beautiful children, aren't they, dear Doctor?"

He put an arm across her shoulders. "Yes, Katharine, of course they are."

"There will be another before long," she announced.

Luther kissed her joyfully. "God be praised!" he said.

By the end of October Katharine was quite heavy and found it difficult to move around. One evening she sat in Luther's study stewing. Hans played with his wooden toys, and baby Lena sat on Luther's lap.

"I think it must be soon, Doctor," Katharine said.

Luther snatched at one of little Lena's hands. "Lenchen!" he cried to the giggling child. "Stop that! Let go of your father's finger." Then he turned to Katharine. "Yes, soon," he said. "What do you want this time, Katharine?"

Katharine looked at Hans and at little Lena and with an ache in her heart thought of baby Elizabeth. "Whatever God sends me," she replied. "What do you want, Doctor?"

"That's easy," Luther laughed. "Another son." He glanced at Hans, who was busily breaking his toys. "An obedient son," he added with a smile.

Two weeks later Katharine gave birth to a son. Luther held him in his arms. "This one is Martin," he announced. "And he shall be a minister of religion."

"A Lutheran minister of religion," Katharine repeated slowly, unaware of the added adjective.

A frown crossed Luther's face. "I said 'a minister of religion,'" he said sternly. "I did not say a Lutheran minister."

Katharine opened her eyes. "I'm sorry. But that's what he'll be, won't he?"

"No!" exploded Luther. "He will not! I have told the people not to call themselves Lutherans. I do not like it, I do not want it. I would rather they called themselves Christians.

I did not die on the cross for their sins, I was not crucified for them."

Katharine had heard all this over and over. "Dear Doctor," she said, "if you're going to get excited about it, perhaps you'd better give the baby to Aunt Lena."

Luther stopped talking and laughed. "Yes, Lord Kate," he said and gave the baby to Aunt Lena. When she had left the room, Luther went to his wife. He knelt beside her bed and kissed her on the forehead. "Again, Katharine, thanks for a son. Thank you, thank you."

Katharine held on to his hand. "You're welcome, dear husband," she said.

Then Luther bowed his head. "Let's give thanks to our God for this wonderful miracle."

$\mathcal{I}$T WAS a hot, sultry day in August, and little Martin was nearing his first birthday. Luther turned to Katharine. "Well," he said, "we again have peace in Germany. The Emperor has been compelled to yield to the demands of the Protestant princes in the matter of religion."

Katharine looked at his tired, drawn face and thought of the long hours he had been working, sometimes far into the night. "I'm glad that we have peace in Germany. God be praised!" she said. Then thoughtfully she left the study and walked out to the garden. Wolf was working with the rosebushes. "Wolf, the doctor is tired," Katharine said.

"Yes, Mistress Luther. He needs a rest."

"He won't rest, but maybe we can give him a little of the next best thing."

Wolf stopped digging and looked at her.

"Maybe we could have a celebration," Katharine said, her eyes growing brighter as the idea took hold.

"A celebration, Mistress Luther?"

"Yes! Tomorrow. I've got plenty of beer on hand, and I'll net some fish. You kill and clean some chickens, and we'll pick fruit. We'll invite all of the doctor's friends and their wives, and we'll play games and sing."

"It would do the doctor good," Wolf said.

"Of course it would. We'll make it a real party."

Early the next morning the town church trumpeter proclaimed the hour, and Katharine was dressed and had prepared breakfast. She sent a messenger with invitations to the party, and she had Wolf fill jugs with beer. Then they walked to the orchard, and while Wolf picked baskets of fruit, Katharine netted fish out of the pond. Her cheeks were flushed, and she pushed aside a damp lock of hair. "Wolf," she called, "don't you think the doctor will be pleased?"

Wolf grinned. "I'm sure of it, Mistress Luther; I'm sure of it."

All day, throughout the sultry heat, Katharine and Wolf and Aunt Lena worked. They baked chickens and fried fish and cleaned fruit. They set up tables under the trees and hung lanterns overhead. Luther remained in his study all day, behind closed doors.

At the evening meal Luther remarked on the scarcity of food. "Why are we having so little food, Katharine? Are we fasting?"

Katharine said in what she hoped was an offhand manner. "Oh, it's too hot to eat."

After devotions and prayers Luther returned to his study, and Katharine and Aunt Lena hastily cleared the table. The guests began arriving, and Katharine met them outside with her finger to her lips. "Sssh," she whispered, "we're going to surprise the doctor."

When they were all assembled under the trees and Wolf had lighted the lanterns, Katharine went in to get Luther. He came out wearing a puzzled frown. When he saw his friends and the lanterns and the long tables piled with food, he grinned. Slowly he walked toward them. He went to each one offering his hand. "The Melanchthons," he said softly as he took their hands, "and Jonas and the Bugenhagens and George Rohrer and Caspar Cruciger and Lucas Cranach." He stopped. "I'm so glad to see all of you." He turned to Katharine. "What's this all about?" he asked.

Katharine laughed. "It's just a party, dear Doctor, just a party."

Then the silence broke, and the guests laughed and joked and went to the food-laden table. They drank toasts to the Emperor, and after eating they played games. Later John Walter, the choirmaster from Torgau, arrived, and they sang folk songs. After the singing a few of the guests left, and those who remained sat and talked in the cool of the evening.

Katharine was sitting under the pear tree with the women when she noticed Spalatin beckoning to her. Going over to him, she asked, "What is it?"

Spalatin glanced over his shoulder and saw that Luther was engaged in conversation. "Here," he said as he pressed some gold pieces into her hand.

Katharine looked at the money. "Ten gold florins!" she gasped. "But Spalatin, where did it come from?"

"It's a gift from the Elector. He knows how much you and the doctor do for others, and he wants to help."

Katharine put the money in her pocket. "God be praised! Thank you, Spalatin." She glanced at Luther, but he was busily engaged in conversation and hadn't seen the transaction.

The party seemed to help Luther. It refreshed and relaxed him for a time, but soon he was absorbed in his busy life and working as hard as ever. He and his colleagues still worked long hours on the difficult task of translating the Bible.

Katharine, too, worked hard, and she did everything she possibly could to make life easier for her husband. She still didn't like the town of Wittenberg and longed for the day when they could leave it.

Some of the church members caused much anguish for Dr. Luther. Katharine tried to do something about it through her contacts with the women, but she wasn't able to accomplish much. The good, pious women were the ones who attended the church services, and the women who were contributing to the low character of the town would, of course, have nothing to do with the church. She knew it grieved her husband — the loud talking in the church, the poor attendance — but she didn't know how she could help. "He does so much for this town," she moaned, "and they accept what he does with no thought of return."

One morning after breakfast Luther turned to Katharine and said, "My heart is sad, and my eyes fill with tears. I can hardly stand it."

"What is it, dear Doctor?"

"Do you remember how last year I did everything I could think of in every possible way to raise the standard of living here in Wittenberg?"

Katharine nodded, remembering.

"I wrote to the Elector, asking him, begging him in fact, to be as a father to my most precious treasure, to take care of the faithful ministers, the young theological students. I asked him to guide and protect them. I wanted him not to shower them with gifts and luxuries, but only to see that they were taken care of."

"I know, Doctor," Katharine said soothingly; "I know that you did all you could."

"I have as many of them at my own table as I can possibly accommodate. I can't do any more myself."

106

"Doctor," Katharine asked, "what has brought on this sudden sad feeling? Have you heard something?"

Luther raised his head. "I have known for a long time that there are many students in Wittenberg that have scarce anything to live on but bread and water. It's a disgrace to this town."

Katharine looked at him with love. "Perhaps one day we'll be able to leave Wittenberg," she said.

"Perhaps. Right now I would gladly wipe the dust of this town off my feet."

Shortly after this Luther received news of the death of his mother. He went to Katharine and said, "O Katharine, I pray that God will not take me and leave you all alone. I hope that I may be allowed to stay and care for you."

Gently Katharine put her hand in his. "You will be with me for a long time to come, dear husband." She watched him as he left the room. The death of his mother, plus the anguish that the people of Wittenberg were causing him, had made his shoulders a little more stooped, his steps a little slower. "He needs one bright ray of happiness," she wished, "something to take his mind off all this." Just a few days later her wish was granted.

Luther came home from church and found Katharine in the kitchen. "Katharine," he said, "I'll never understand how you can sit in church looking every bit a lady of leisure, and by the time I get home you're already in the kitchen hard at work."

"That's not hard to understand," she said as she kept on working. "I've got just so much work to do and so many hours in which to do it. I have to hurry."

"I got a raise in salary today," Luther said, "and Elector John has officially confirmed the grant made by Elector Frederick the Wise before he died, so that now the parsonage is legally deeded to us."

Katharine stopped her work. "And you accepted?" she asked.

"Of course I did! A laborer is worthy of his hire!"

"God be praised!" was all Katharine could say.

Later that same morning, as Katharine worked in the kitchen, a thought came to her. She went to her husband. "Dear Doctor," she began, "do you suppose we could possibly purchase the small garden next to the parsonage?"

"Why? You're using it now, aren't you?"

Katharine twisted the ends of her apron. "Yes, dear Doctor, but now that we own the parsonage, don't you think we should own the garden too?"

Luther stared at her. "That doesn't make good sense."

Katharine twisted her apron harder. "Please, Doctor, it does make good sense."

Luther stood. He scowled. "Stop twisting your apron, Katharine, and look at me!" he said.

Katharine buried her face in her hands and fled from the room. She controlled her tears and went on with her work. However, everyone in the house knew that something was wrong by the way she slammed and banged her way through her chores. That evening, as they were undressing for bed, Luther said casually, "Oh, by the way, I purchased the garden you wanted."

Katharine stopped for an instant and then rushed into his arms.

"Now why are you crying?" Luther asked. "I thought you wanted the garden."

"I did — I mean, I do," Katharine sobbed, "but I'm so mean and selfish, I don't deserve to have it."

Luther stroked her hair. "Yes, you do, Katharine; you deserve that and much more."

When she had stopped crying, Luther said, "While I was

at it, I also purchased the large house and property of Claus Bildenhauer on the Swine Market."

Katharine looked at him in amazement. "Doesn't the lazy brook flow through that property?" she asked.

Luther nodded.

"I can fish there?"

"It's yours now. You can do anything you like."

"O dear Doctor," she said, "I love you very much. You're a dear, generous husband."

Luther smiled. "No," he said softly, "I'm just intelligent enough to appreciate a good wife when I have one."

chapter fifteen

$\mathcal{I}$T WAS JANUARY 1533, and the last traces of the Christmas holidays had been removed. Katharine was glad to rest. "Dear Doctor," she said one morning, "I think that it will be soon that you will again be a father."

Luther looked at her. "Yes, soon," he said, "very soon." Then he took her in his arms. "You must rest. I don't want you to be ill."

She touched his hand. "I feel fine, Doctor. Just a little tired, is all."

"Then you will rest," he declared, "and I shall see to it." He looked into her eyes. "Do you suppose, dear wife, that God will bless us with another daughter?"

Katharine shrugged her shoulders. "Does it really matter?" she asked.

Just a few weeks later, January 28, Luther again held a son in his arms. "This one is Paul," he announced, "a good Biblical name."

Katharine laughed. "Go and have the little heathen baptized, dear Doctor, and let me sleep."

With a roar of laughter Luther left the room.

The year 1533 passed swiftly, and Katharine was grateful for Aunt Lena's help in caring for the children. She was at first dismayed when she learned that she was again expecting a child. However, as the time drew near, she thanked God over and over for the blessing of a large family. On December 17, 1534, she again gave birth to a child. Luther was overjoyed because it was a daughter. "O Katharine," he said, "you have given me another daughter!"

He held the baby in his arms and rocked her to and fro. "She can never replace baby Elizabeth, but we again have a daughter."

"Doctor! You talk as if we didn't have little Lena."

"That precious one? No, I'm just happy to have another daughter."

Katharine turned her head. "What shall we name her, Doctor?"

Luther frowned. "I don't know. I'm at a loss for a name. What name would you like, Katharine?"

"I had thought of Margaret."

Luther bounced the tiny bundle in his arms. "Margaret she shall be," he laughed.

Luther had finished his translation of the Bible — a mountainous piece of work on which he and Melanchthon and others had put in long, weary hours of work. Katharine rejoiced with them when the translation was completed, and in her heart she hoped that now Luther would have a little more time to himself.

On Hans's ninth birthday Katharine persuaded Luther to join in a birthday celebration in the summer house. He readily agreed but told them to go down, and he would be along shortly.

They left immediately and soon were there. Hans and little Lena played near the flowing Elbe, Katharine sat with baby Margaret in her lap, Aunt Lena dozed in the sun, and

Wolf kept a watchful eye on the children. They were waiting for Luther and knew that the party wouldn't begin until he came. Presently Wolf called to Katharine that he and Hans were going to take a stroll into the woods. A few minutes after they had left, Luther arrived. "Where's Hans?" he asked. "Where's our birthday boy?"

"He and Wolf took a stroll into the woods," Katharine answered. "They'll be back soon."

Luther played a game of hide and seek with Lena. Martin and Paul played gleefully with their father, stumbling around on short, fat legs.

When Hans and Wolf returned, Hans rushed to his father. "Papa," he said, "we've been waiting for you."

Luther grabbed his son and held him in the air. "What were you doing that was so important to take you away from your own party?" he asked.

Immediately Hans's face fell. He glanced at Wolf and then back to his father. Slowly Luther put the boy down. All eyes were on Hans, who stared at the tips of his shoes.

"What were you doing, Hans?" Luther repeated.

In a small voice Hans answered, "We were trying to trap birds."

Luther looked at Hans for long minutes. The only sound was the rushing of the river behind them. Then he turned to Katharine. "I have forbidden the boy to trap poor, defenseless birds, which are God's creatures. I will not speak to him all day."

Katharine was dismayed. "Doctor," she pleaded, "I'm sure that he's sorry and will not do it again." She glanced at Hans. "Besides," she added, "it's his birthday."

Luther sat down next to Aunt Lena. "Nevertheless," he said in a firm voice, "I do not intend to speak to him again today."

Little Lena rushed to Hans and threw her arms around him. She whispered in his ear and then gently pushed him toward Luther. Hans stood before his father. "I'm sorry, Papa, and I won't do it again," he said. Luther ignored him and talked to Katharine. Hans walked slowly away and sat on the grass.

Little Lena ran to her father and threw herself into his lap. Her slender body shook. "Please, Papa, don't do this to Hans. Please! Please!" she sobbed.

Luther stroked her hair. "Why not, little Lena?"

"Because I can't bear it," she cried. "It's cruel, Papa, cruel!"

"Don't you think Hans was being cruel to the little birds?"

"Yes, Papa, but he's truly sorry, and he won't do it again."

"How do we know that he won't? I had already forbidden him to do it. Yet he did it again."

Little Lena reached a hand up and stroked Luther's cheek. "Papa, I know that he won't ever do it again, because Hans is really a good boy," she said softly.

Luther smiled and took her hand in his. "You love your brother very much, don't you, little Lena?"

"Yes, Papa, I do. Hans is good to me. I love everyone though, Papa, because God wants me to."

Luther glanced at Katharine. "This little one can wrap me around her little finger," he said. Then he turned to Hans. "Come here, son," he said. Hans rushed to him.

The birthday celebration, although somewhat subdued, continued until dusk. Then Wolf went to Luther. "Begging your pardon, Doctor, the physician forbids you the night air. We'd best be going home."

"I have so many people leading me around by the nose," Luther growled, "I can't call myself master of my own household." They all laughed and started down the road toward the parsonage.

That evening, when the children were asleep, Katharine and her husband sat in his study for a few minutes of quiet talk. The rare moments of tranquillity were peaceful little islands for them to look forward to. Katharine sighed and looked at Luther. "It was a very pleasant day, wasn't it, dear Doctor?" she asked.

He ran a hand through his hair. "Yes, Katharine, a very pleasant day," he answered. "However, I think I enjoy even more these few minutes with you at the end of a day."

Katharine smiled. Then Luther rose. "Soon," he said, "I'll have to be making another trip."

Katharine raised her eyebrows. "O Doctor," she said, "you're not well enough to make another trip."

"I'm just tired," he answered, "that's all. The Elector wants me to go to Smalkald. I think that I must go."

Immediately Katharine started fussing about people making too many demands on him.

Luther took her into his arms.

"Let's go to bed, dear wife. We're both tired. We'll discuss this in the morning."

A few weeks later Katharine awoke at dawn and instantly felt a surge of fear. "This is the day he leaves," she thought. Hurriedly, she dressed and went down to the kitchen, where Wolf was eating a solitary breakfast.

"Good morning, Mistress Luther," he mumbled. "This is the day the doctor leaves."

Katharine looked into his eyes. "He loves him as much as I do," she thought. She touched a hand on his shoulder. "Yes, Wolf, and we must be certain that he is warm and comfortable for the trip."

114

Wolf finished his meal as Katharine bustled about the kitchen. As he was shuffling out of the room, Katharine said, "We'll let the doctor sleep this morning, Wolf, as long as he will."

Wolf turned to her. "He's been up for some time now, Mistress Luther. He's in his study."

Impatiently Katharine ran to Luther's study. Without knocking she rushed in. He sat at his desk, his head laid wearily on his arms. Tenderly she went to him and touched his hand. "Dear Doctor," she said, "you're sick and you're tired. Why must you make this trip? How could the Elector be so inconsiderate as to insist that you do this? He knows how sick you are."

Luther raised his head and, rubbing his eyes, said, "It's necessary, Katharine, or he wouldn't have asked me to go."

Katharine sighed and walked to the door. "If by chance you should die as a result of this ill-advised trip, it would plunge the whole Protestant world into confusion. Does that make sense?"

Luther smiled wanly. "Katharine, no man, not even Martin Luther, is that important."

She left the room and returned to the kitchen. Soon she heard the rattle of carriage wheels. She hurried to the door, where Wolf greeted her with a proud smile. "The Elector sent his own carriage for the doctor," he said.

"Why didn't he also send along some magic potion to make the good doctor well?" Katharine said.

Luther came slowly down the stairs and allowed Wolf to help him into the carriage. Katharine ran out with a fur robe, which she tucked securely around him. "Here is some medicine," she said as she handed him a bottle. "Be sure and take it. Take good care of yourself, and don't get overtired. Be sure and keep warm and don't forget —"

Luther interrupted her. "Lord Kate!"

She stopped her chattering and looked into his eyes. "If I don't do something," she said, "I'll cry."

The anguish in her eyes was so real that Luther leaned down and pulled her up to the seat beside him. He wrapped his arm around her and held her trembling body close for a few seconds.

"Katharine," he said, "what does your husband always say to you at times like this?"

Katharine looked down. "I know, I know."

Luther gently lifted her face to his. "What is it, Katharine?" he urged. "What is it that I always say to you?"

With a weak smile Katharine said, "God will watch over you. He is everywhere with you."

"Thank you, Katharine. Thank you. And now I must be on my way."

Katharine stepped down from the carriage and waved as Luther moved away and headed out of town. When the last cloud of dust had rolled away, she impatiently brushed away a tear and turned to Wolf. "We've got lots of work to do, Wolf. Let's get busy."

A month passed, and Katharine received no word from Luther. She became increasingly worried, and others noticed that she was becoming nervous and silent. On March 2 a messenger brought a letter from Luther. Wolf brought the letter to her. He stood before her, delight written across his face. "I have a letter from the doctor," he said.

Immediately Katharine dropped her sewing. "Give it to me, Wolf, quickly!"

Wolf watched her face as she read. When she gasped and turned pale, he asked, "What's wrong, Mistress Luther?"

Katharine tried to control her shaking voice. "He's been

close to death. He says here that he was so sick he thought he was going to die."

Wolf shook his head. "He should never have gone. You're the only one that knows how to care for him. If you had been with him, he would have been all right."

"That's it, Wolf!" she said. "That's it! I must go to him. I'll nurse him back to health and then bring him home."

"The doctor took the horses," Wolf said. "The Elector sent his own carriage, but the doctor took his own horses."

"Then hire some and get our carriage ready. I'll leave in the morning. He'll be in Altenburg, and I'll meet him there. In the meantime I'll get a message off to Spalatin to tell him that I'm coming."

The next day Katharine arrived at Altenburg and went immediately to Spalatin's home. Spalatin met her at the door. "The doctor is coming," he told her.

Katharine waited impatiently until Luther arrived the next day. As he was being helped out of the carriage, he saw Katharine waiting at the door. A smile creased his face. "Somehow I knew you'd be here," he said.

During the next few days Katharine carefully nursed her husband back to health. She was relentless in keeping people away from him so that he could rest. Soon, feeling better, he and Katharine rode back to Wittenberg. As they entered the town, Katharine reached for Luther's hand. "God has been good to me, my dear children, and Aunt Lena," she said, "and He has spared you, my dear husband."

In answer, Luther smiled and patted her hand.

$\mathcal{L}$IFE RETURNED to normal in the parsonage, and Katharine worked even harder than ever to see that the burden on Luther was eased. One morning, several weeks after Luther's return from Smalkald, Aunt Lena put her hand to her eyes. "Katharine," she said in a low voice, "I think I'll lie down for a little while." Luther and Katharine gently helped her to her room, and Katharine put her to bed. "Is there anything I can bring you, Aunt Lena?" she asked. Aunt Lena shook her head. "Don't look so worried, Katharine. I'm old, and I'm entitled to feel tired once in a while."

Katharine sent the children out to play and asked Wolf to keep an eye on them. She went about her duties in a half-hearted way and frequently peeked in on Aunt Lena. At noon Aunt Lena refused food, saying that she was too tired to eat. The day wore on, and still she slept. In the evening Katharine put the children to bed and then sat at Lena's bedside. In a short time Aunt Lena opened her eyes. "Katharine," she whispered, "would you ask the good doctor to come in here?"

Katharine rushed to Luther's study and returned with him in a few seconds. They stood at her bedside, and Aunt Lena smiled. "Good Sir Doctor, will you pray for my soul?"

Luther knelt at her side, made the sign of the cross, and began praying. Katharine walked to the window and stood with her back to them, but she prayed silently along with her husband. Luther stopped after a few minutes, and Katharine stiffened. "She's gone, Katharine," Luther said. "She's left us to be with her Lord."

Katharine turned and walked into Luther's outstretched arms. "She has always been like a mother to me," she sobbed.

"We've lost a good friend," Luther said.

Katharine missed Aunt Lena more and more as the months passed. She didn't realize until Aunt Lena was gone how much she had depended on her. However, she soon had something else which occupied her thoughts. Luther had complained over the years of a pain in his stomach. The doctor had told him it was the stones. One cold, raw day in February Katharine went into his study and found him at his desk in great pain.

"What's wrong, Doctor?" she asked.

"I don't know, Katharine, but I'm in great pain." He held his hands across his stomach.

Quickly Katharine lighted a fire in the fireplace and pulled a chair close to it. She helped him into the chair and brought him a glass of wine. "Sip this," she said, "and I'll get Physician Schurf."

Luther stopped her. "Katharine, send one of the servants for Doctor Schurf. You stay near me."

When Dr. Schurf arrived, he had Luther put to bed. "Katharine," he announced, "it's the stones again."

"I was afraid of that," Katharine said.

Luther remained in bed for several days. Finally one day, when she asked him if he was feeling any better, he replied, "Much better; the pain is gone."

Katharine stayed by his side until he fell asleep. Then she said a prayer of thanksgiving and got up to get the evening meal for the children. Luther recovered, but Katharine grew more and more worried about his health. One day she said to him, "Dear Doctor, can't we buy a little place in the country?"

Luther looked at her in amazement. "Why in the world would we want a little place in the country?"

Katharine smiled. "I know it must sound foolish to you, dear Doctor, but I have always wanted a place like that. Also, it would be a nice little peaceful place for us to go to at times where you could rest and regain your strength."

Luther laughed. "When could I find time to go to a place in the country?" he asked.

"We would find the time if we had the place."

"Why do you really want this?" he asked.

"Well, when I was in the convent, I saw a bird flying and I — "

"You saw a bird flying? What does that have to do with this?"

Katharine bit her lip. "Oh, nothing. I just thought that it would be a good idea for us to have a sort of refuge. Some place where we could go to get away from the parsonage once in a while. A place where we could eventually retire." She left the room as soon as she finished speaking. She had so hoped that he would agree with her and want to buy a place, but it looked as though he didn't even know what she was talking about.

Several days later her brother Hans and his wife visited them. They were dressed in fine clothes and drove up in a beautiful carriage. The Luther children were impressed and hovered around them. Never had they seen such lovely materials as their visitors wore. While Katharine prepared a lunch for them, Luther and Hans walked around the grounds.

Then, several days after Hans's visit, Luther said to Katharine, "I've got a surprise for you."

"What is it, dear Doctor?"

"Don't ask questions, but get ready for a trip. We'll go and look at it."

Wondering, Katharine packed some things and got into the carriage with Luther, Wolf doing the driving. Two days later they reached Zulsdorf, the von Bora estate that belonged to Katharine's brother. It had been in the von Bora family for years, and Katharine herself had lived there until her mother's death, when she had been sent to the convent.

"Here it is," Luther said, "and it's all yours!"

Tears streaked down Katharine's cheeks. He had known what she was talking about after all!

The grounds were overrun with weeds, and the house itself, although a fine house, was in need of repair. Wolf grunted, "I don't know why anyone would want this place."

Katharine laughed. "You just wait and see what I do with it. Then you'll love it too. It will be a wonderful haven of rest for the dear doctor."

Luther grinned. "And also a place where the dear doctor's wife can feel free as a bird," he teased.

Katharine was anxious to start work on the beautifying of Zulsdorf, but she wouldn't go there so long as her husband was at home and needed her. In the meantime she was working too hard now, doing all the things that for years Aunt Lena had taken over for her. One morning she awoke with a strange weakness. When she tried to get up, she found she was too weak to raise her head. When she didn't appear for breakfast, Luther hurried to her room. He entered the bedroom, a worried frown creasing his face. "Katharine, what's wrong?"

She turned her face toward him and found it was an effort even to do that. "Doctor," she whispered, "I'm sick. Please get the physician."

In a short time Dr. Schurf was at her bedside. Luther stayed by his side. After a few minutes Dr. Schurf beckoned to Luther to follow him, and they left the room. In the hallway Luther grabbed Dr. Schurf by the arm. "What's wrong with her? What is it?"

Dr. Schurf shrugged his shoulders. "I don't know what it is, Martin," he answered slowly. "She's tired of course, exhausted in fact. But that isn't all." He stopped and glanced at Luther. "I wonder whether she's still grieving over the death of Aunt Lena?"

Luther sighed. "What can I do for her?"

"Keep her in bed. She must rest. And cheer her. Don't let her become upset or unhappy."

For the next two weeks Katharine lay in bed. She ate and drank only what was practically forced down her throat. She slept most of the time.

When Dr. Schurf came again, he told Luther, "I'm sorry, Martin, dear friend, but I see no hope for her. There is nothing I can do."

Luther looked at him with horror in his eyes. "This can't be true!" he cried. "I won't believe it. It can't be that I'm to lose my wife." Great tears rolled down his cheeks.

With a sad shake of his head the physician left, and Luther went to his wife's side. He knelt beside her bed and took one of her thin hands in his. "Katharine," he said, "Katharine, there is nothing that anyone can do for you. No one except your husband, who loves you greatly. I am going to beg God to spare you, my dearest, because I love you and need you so much." All through that night Luther stayed at Katharine's side and prayed aloud. When dawn broke, he stopped. His voice was hoarse, and he was tired beyond belief.

122

He sat in a chair in a corner of the room and fell asleep. When he woke, several hours later, he saw Katharine trying to sit up. He rushed to her. "Katharine! Are you feeling better?"

She smiled. "I want to try and sit up, dear Doctor," she said. Luther held her in his arms. "Thank God!" he said over and over. Katharine ran her hand over his lined face. "Dear Doctor, you prayed for me last night, didn't you?"

Luther nodded.

"You begged God to spare my life because you love me and need me?"

Again Luther nodded.

"I thought it was true, not a dream. Some strength came to me from somewhere."

"Katharine, you had given up. You weren't trying to recover."

"I know, dear Doctor, but I'll be all right now."

Luther kissed her and said, "Katharine, you don't know how much I love you."

"May I have some food?" she asked.

Within a few days she was out of bed. By hanging on to tables and chairs she crept around the house. In a few weeks she was again well and strong, up at dawn each morning, cooking meals and caring for Luther and the children and working in her garden. Luther smiled as he watched her. "My morning star of Wittenberg has risen again," he said.

That spring Luther asked Katharine why she didn't go to Zulsdorf. "You love the place so much," he said. "I don't see why you and the children don't go now and spend the spring and summer there."

"No," Katharine answered. "I can't go. Not at this time."

"Why?"

"Why?" Katharine looked at him. "Hans and Martin must stay here because of their studies," she answered.

Luther rubbed his chin. "There's something peculiar about this," he said. "I know how much you'd like to go to Zulsdorf. It isn't because of Hans and Martin. You and Paul and Margaret could go, and little Lena. Hans and Martin are old enough to take care of themselves. What's the real reason?"

Katharine shrugged her shoulders. "It's not hard to figure out. I am not the kind of woman to go away seeking pleasure while my husband is at home. That's all there is to it."

Luther took her in his arms. "I am surely blessed to have a wife like you," he said.

However, in July Luther went to Hagenau, and Katharine, Paul, Margaret, and little Lena left the same day for Zulsdorf. As she left, she gave final instructions to Hans and Martin and their tutors and added, "Now remember, when your father returns, you are all three to join us in Zulsdorf."

Feeling quite grown up, the boys stuck out their chests. "Yes, Mother," they answered. "We'll join you then."

Katharine and her children arrived at Zulsdorf in the late afternoon. The children, with squeals of delight, ran around the grounds and threw pebbles into the stream. Katharine stood on the lawn, looking at the beautiful cottage nestled among the trees and flowers. "It's such a lovely place," she thought. In comparison with the hot, dusty streets of Wittenberg, Zulsdorf was like a garden of Eden, green and cool and serene.

A few days after their arrival Katharine received a letter from Luther. She read it to the children. "Your father says that Melanchthon was ill, near to death, but is now recovering." As she read on, she smiled and said, "Children, listen to this letter." She read: "Monday after St. James' Day, 1540. To

124

the Lady of Zulsdorf, my Love: Tomorrow morning, on Tuesday, we purpose to leave this place. The Diet at Hagenau has accomplished nothing. Labor and time and money have been wasted. Yet, even though we have done little else, we have drawn Master Philip from the grave, and will bring him home in good health, if it be God's will. Amen. Your lover, Martin Luther."

"Mother," Paul asked, "will Father and the boys be able to find us here?"

Katharine smiled. "They will find us," she said.

Three days later the children, who each day had climbed the hill behind the house to look down the road, observed a cloud of dust in the distance. As it came nearer, they saw it was a coach. "Father's coming!" Paul shouted. "Father's coming home!"

The coach pulled up in front of the house, and Luther and his sons got out. They were dusty and tired. Katharine greeted them, "Dear Doctor, I have so many things to show you. We've done so much to Zulsdorf."

"Katharine, my dear," Luther replied. "We are dirty and hungry and tired. May we wash, eat, and sleep first? Then we'll admire the things that you have done to Zulsdorf."

After Luther and the children were all in bed napping, Katharine returned to the large living room and started a fire in the fireplace. She seated herself in front of it and waited. In a short while Luther joined her. "Doctor," she asked, "have you had enough sleep?"

"Yes, Katharine. The children are still sleeping, and I want to talk to you alone."

He settled himself comfortably next to her and held her hand. For a while he stared absently into the fire. Then he turned to her. "Katharine, I wish that I could leave Wittenberg."

At that moment a log in the fire crackled, and Katharine jumped. "Dear Doctor," she said, "do you know what you're saying?"

Luther sighed and rubbed a hand across his forehead. "Yes, my dear. I wish I could leave Wittenberg and come to Zulsdorf to live."

Katharine squeezed his hand. "O Doctor, I wish you could." Then she added, "Why do you want to leave?"

Luther looked away. "The people in Wittenberg have no respect for their church any more. They talk and chatter during the service. The young people are rowdy. I can't stand any more of that sort of thing."

"I know," Katharine said softly. "You have tried to make the people see that they are being rude and sacrilegious; it's been a great trial to you."

He turned to her. "My dear wife, in a few days I'm going to make a short trip. I want you and the children to stay here, and we'll have a long vacation. I've already written Melanchthon and told him about my plans. While I am gone, I want you to rest and relax, and I'll be back in a short time."

"Yes, dear Doctor," she answered. "It will be wonderful to have a long vacation."

At that moment the children rushed in and tumbled into Luther's lap. Over their heads Katharine looked at her husband.

The next few days at Zulsdorf were days filled with happiness for Katharine. She and Luther and the children wandered over the grounds, and Luther was lavish in his praise of all that Katharine had done. Next door to the estate was another piece of property named Wachsdorf.

"That is a beautiful piece of property," Luther said.

"Do you think so, Doctor?" Katharine asked.

"Why, don't you like it?"

"Yes, Doctor, I like it, but I'm so happy and contented with Zulsdorf and with having you and our children here, that I can think of nothing else."

Luther put an arm around her. "You never did like Wittenberg, did you, Katharine?"

"Well, I guess I didn't think it very pretty or —"

"You never liked it, did you?" Luther insisted.

Katharine hung her head. "No, Doctor," she replied. "I never did."

Hans joined them. "What are my dear parents talking about so earnestly?" he asked.

"Son," Luther said, "one of these days we're going to buy Wachsdorf too. Zulsdorf and Wachsdorf together will someday make a nice inheritance for the Luther children."

"It is pretty, Father. However, I'll not have much use for it."

"Why not?" Katharine asked.

Hans stuck out his chest. "I'll be a great lawyer, don't forget."

Katharine smiled and patted his arm, and Luther put an arm across the boy's thin shoulders. "Hans, we are very proud of you," he said.

As they started for the house, Paul ran up to them. "Mother! Father!" he cried excitedly. "A carriage is coming down the road!"

Katharine laughed. "Don't get so excited, Paul. When they get here, we'll find out who it is."

When the carriage pulled up in front of the house, Katharine was dismayed to see that it was Melanchthon and Reuter. "I know why they've come," she thought. "I know why, and I pray that — " She stopped and hung her head. "God's will be done," she whispered resignedly. She straightened her dress and went to greet them.

Inside the house Luther stood with his back to the fireplace, and the two visitors faced him. Katharine walked to the window opposite and stood with her back to the room.

"Brother Martin," Melanchthon began, "we don't like to interrupt your much-needed vacation, but we would like to have you return immediately to Wittenberg."

Reuter spoke. "All of your congregation asked me to tell you that they want you to hurry back."

"You are their pastor, Brother Martin," Melanchthon said. "They need you."

Luther growled. "When I was there, I asked them over and over to mend their ways. I begged and pleaded with them."

"We know all that," Reuter said, "and now they are sorry and have promised me that if you return soon they will in the future conduct themselves as Christians should."

Katharine stayed at the window and didn't dare look at her husband. Nervously she twisted the ends of the curtain in her fingers.

Then Melanchthon spoke into the silence. "If you do not return, Brother Martin, I shall leave Wittenberg also."

There was a long silence, and then Katharine heard Luther's voice. "I intended to return, of course. But not so soon." He shrugged his shoulders. "As God pleases."

Katharine whirled to face him.

"I'm sorry," he said, looking into her eyes. "It is God's will."

Katharine stifled her tears and walked over to Melanchthon and Reuter. "Be seated, gentlemen," she said in a tight voice. "I'll bring refreshments."

128

A few days later, as their carriage passed the Elster Gate and entered Wittenberg, Katharine looked down at the muddy streets and sighed. Luther leaned over and patted her hand. "It is God's will, Katharine," he said.

Katharine nodded. "Yes, dear Doctor. I understand."

$\mathcal{K}$ATHARINE was not happy about returning to Wittenberg, but since it had to be, she tried to make the best of it. She enjoyed the companionship of her children. Hans was old enough now to make some of the trips with his father, and Katharine enjoyed being with little Lena. Although the child was only twelve years old, she was a real companion to her mother. Katharine was determined to make their lives happy, even though they had to live in Wittenberg. She dreamed of the day when they would retire to Zulsdorf.

In the late summer of 1542 Hans went to Torgau to visit friends, and Katharine and little Lena were enjoying a rare moment of relaxation one afternoon. They were sitting under the pear tree in the front yard. Katharine's hands were busy with her sewing, and little Lena played with her dolls. Katharine contemplated her happiness, and the warmth of the sun felt good. She looked at little Lena's blond curls glinting in the sunlight and smiled. Suddenly, the girl looked at her mother. Her eyes were wide with fear. "Mother," she gasped, "I don't feel well."

Katharine dropped her sewing and ran to the child. "Lena! What's wrong? You're so pale!"

Lena put a hand to her chest. Her eyes were dark pools in the whiteness of her face. "My chest," she panted. "It hurts."

Katharine quickly carried little Lena into the house and put her to bed. Dr. Schurf arrived and spent a long time examining the child. Finally he turned to Luther and Katharine. "It's serious," he said, "but I don't know what it is." He looked at them helplessly. "I don't know what to do for her."

The next few days dragged, and Katharine, sitting by Lena's bedside, didn't know day from night. She knew that Lena was in pain, but the child didn't cry. Her pain was evident only in the cruel, torturous grimacing on her face. One morning she raised her head and asked, "Father, I want to see Hans. Will you send to Torgau for him, please?"

Anxious to do anything she wished, and glad for the opportunity to do something, Luther sent Wolf to Torgau to bring Hans home. Two days later Hans arrived. When he walked into the parsonage, Katharine ran to him.

"Mother," he said, "thank God you're all right." Then he held her at arm's length. "What's wrong, Mother? Why did you send for me? Wolf wouldn't tell me a thing."

Silently Katharine led him to Lena's room. "She's very, very sick," she whispered. "She asked for you."

Hans dropped to his knees and took his little sister in his arms. Quietly Katharine left the room.

That night Luther persuaded Katharine to lie down. "Try to sleep," he said gently. "Perhaps having Hans here has done more good than we know."

Katharine lay down and fell into a troubled sleep. When she awoke, a few hours later, Melanchthon and Luther were talking in the study. Katharine rushed to them. "I had a dream," she said. "I thought I saw little Lena, radiant with

131

light, floating on a cloud and two elegantly dressed youths came to lead her to the marriage feast." Her eyes shone as she told them of the dream. She looked from Luther to Melanchthon. "It's a good omen," she said. "Nothing is impossible with God."

When she had left the room, Melanchthon smiled sadly and turned to Luther. "Do you read the vision thus, Martin?" he asked. "I would not take from your wife her hope, but knowing that you have already yielded the dear child to the Lord, I will tell you what I take its meaning to be. The youths are blessed angels who will lead the maiden into the heavenly kingdom, to the true Bridegroom."

Outside the door Katharine bit deep into her knuckles. She felt as if there were a huge scream inside her, welling up like a wave just before it reaches the shore and breaks. She ran down the hall to Lena's room.

Later Luther came to Lena's room. She was feverish and writhing in pain. He took her in his arms. "Magdalene, my little daughter," he spoke into her ear, "you are content to go to your Father above?"

Lena lay very still in his arms. "Yes, dear Father," she whispered. "As God pleases."

Katharine was kneeling on the other side of the bed. Her sobs were the only sound in the room.

"Katharine, Katharine!" Luther pleaded. "Remember where she is going."

Katharine buried her face in her hands and tried in vain to swallow her tears.

Lena's pains seemed to grow worse, and then even Luther's strength left him. He cried bitterly. "O Lord, have mercy, and end her suffering!" Lena gave a final, agonizing twitch of pain and then breathed her last.

After a few minutes Luther stumbled out of the room and saw Paul and Hans and Martin and Margaret waiting with questioning looks. Blindly, without a word, he walked to his study. When he was gone, the children again turned toward their sister's door. A maid came out then and looked at them with pity in her eyes. "You no longer have your sister," she said.

They stared at her, unbelieving. The maid ran down the hall. Still they waited, their eyes glued to the door. Then their mother came out and stood in front of them. They searched her face for an answer. She didn't say a word, but then the children knew. Lena was dead! Katharine silently gathered them all in her arms and wept. After a few minutes she straightened and held her head high. "I shall go in now and prepare my daughter for her funeral," she said. "See that I'm not disturbed." She went into Lena's room and closed the door.

The funeral was held three days later. Katharine had dressed the child and brushed her golden curls. Now she placed a bunch of fresh flowers in her cold hands. Crowds of people waited outside as the coffin was brought out and placed under the pear tree. Luther walked up to the casket and looked down at his daughter's lifeless face. "Thou dear child," he said, "it is well with thee." He turned to the crowd watching him. In a choked voice he addressed them. "I am glad that she is in heaven; my sorrow is all of the flesh."

After the service was over and Lena was buried next to baby Elizabeth, the Luthers went to the parsonage. As they walked toward the house, Luther said, "Ah, Katharine, children are a source of great anxiety, and especially the poor girls. One does not so much fear for boys, they can manage to make a living, they are able to work; but girls can scarce do anything but beg. A boy can go to school and acquire learning, by which he may live; a girl has no such opportunity, and

133

the chances are that she turns to evil courses. 'Tis therefore all the more resignedly that I give my poor little girl to the Lord." Inside the house, Luther held his weeping wife in his arms. "Our little daughter is at rest," he said, "both in body and soul. We Christians should not murmur, knowing that it must be thus and being sure of eternal life; for God's promise, given through His dear Son, cannot fail."

"Ah, you are a strong man," Katharine said, "but a mother is a weak and timid thing. God will have patience with me. I will not murmur."

"Weep freely, dearest," Luther said. "Weep freely."

Time, Katharine knew, would ease their sorrow, but the loss of her daughter was a cruel blow, and it took a great effort to return to a normal life. Every day some new thing reminded her of little Lena, and she had to fight the tears. In an effort to ease the pain she concentrated more and more on her sons. She and Luther had decided to let Jerome Weller, a bright young student at the university, tutor the boys. So far it had worked out to everyone's satisfaction.

One spring morning Katharine worked in her garden. Already the sun was hot, and she had been working since breakfast. Hans came out to her. "Mother, may I help you in the garden?" he asked.

Katharine leaned on her hoe and looked at her son. "Where's Jerome? You should be at your lessons."

Hans stuck out his narrow chest. "Jerome said I'm doing fine, Mother. He gave me the rest of the day to myself."

Surprised, Katharine asked, "Hans, are you really doing better in your studies?"

"Yes, Mother, really," Hans grinned.

Katharine's eyes flicked over his thin body. "Now, if you

were only more robust, your father's joy would be complete," she said.

Hans knelt down and began pulling weeds. "I think he'll be happy, Mother," he said as he tossed weeds over his shoulder. "I'm going to have a talk with him tonight."

Katharine dug her hoe into the earth. "What about, Hans?"

The boy stopped his work and looked into his mother's eyes. "I want to attend the university," he said seriously.

Katharine gasped. "The university! Why, Hans?"

"Mother, I'm sixteen years old, and other boys my age are attending the university."

"But do you think you're ready for it?"

"Jerome Weller says I am, and he ought to know."

"Perhaps," Katharine answered. "However, this is a very important decision to make, and your father and I will have to give it some thought."

"I hope you'll decide to let me attend," Hans said hopefully.

Katharine continued to work. She felt a little sad, knowing that her son was growing into manhood so quickly. Hans picked up a hoe and went to work. Katharine looked at him and then said, "We'll see what your father says this evening. In the meantime keep after those weeds!"

Luther was as surprised as Katharine had been to learn that Hans wanted to enter the university. However, after he and Katharine had discussed the matter, he talked to Hans's tutor and then discussed it with some of the university professors. Finally he told Hans that he might enter the university of Wittenberg. Hans did surprisingly well, and one day Katharine heard Luther mutter, "The boy is really outgrowing his childish ways, isn't he?"

That evening, during family devotions, Luther said to the children, and particularly to Hans: "Children, read your Bible. Listen eagerly whenever anyone reads it to you. I was twenty years old before I had even seen the Bible. I had no notion that there existed any other Gospels or Epistles than those read in the service."

He glanced at each one of the children and then continued, "Dr. Usinger, an Augustinian monk, used to find me reading the Bible, and once he said to me, 'Ah, Brother Martin, why trouble yourself with the Bible? Rather read the ancient doctors who have collected together for you all this marrow and honey. The Bible itself is the cause of all our troubles.'" Luther sighed, remembering.

$\mathcal{L}$IFE WENT ON in the parsonage, but Katharine dreamed more and more of Zulsdorf. Every time she looked at the muddy streets and the shabby buildings, she longed for the Luther family to be enjoying the cool serenity of Zulsdorf. She was also concerned about Luther's health. He had worked hard for long years, and now he was tired. She felt that life in the country would be good for him. Also, she felt that she and Luther had served others for a long time, that now they should be allowed to live out their remaining years together in peace and quiet.

One evening, as they sat together in his study, Luther rose and walked slowly across the room. He dropped into a chair and wearily rubbed his eyes with the tips of his fingers. "I am desirous of leaving this life, Katharine," he said. "I am old and overwhelmed with weariness."

Katharine looked at him and for a brief instant wanted to hold him in her arms and let the warmth and energy of her body flow into his. Instead, she said, "Please don't talk like that, Doctor."

Luther sighed, and in the wake of his sigh there was a deep, thinking silence.

"If you and I left Wittenberg," Katharine said, "and went to Zulsdorf, we would be warm and comfortable and happy, and life would be so different for you."

Luther looked at her through narrowed eyes. "I am old and sick," he said. "Why would it be any different at Zulsdorf?"

Katharine's eyes sparkled, and she leaned forward. "Because at Zulsdorf we would find our dream's end, dear Doctor. When we looked out the window, we would see flowers and trees and cool, green loveliness. We wouldn't have a daily stream of people coming to our door taking your time and attention. We would have time to sit and talk and let the silent beauty of Zulsdorf be absorbed into our very blood. We'd be renewed, Doctor."

Luther looked at her eager face. Her slim body was strained forward in eagerness. "I'm sorry, Katharine," he said. "I'm so very sorry."

Katharine leaned back, and a weariness crept over her and showed in her face. "Why are you sorry?" she asked.

"Because this dream means so much to you, and I have kept it from you. I've kept it dangling in front of you as one dangles a sweet in front of a child, but I've never let you really have it."

Katharine rose. "Dear Doctor, you have not kept me from it. In your great generosity you bought Zulsdorf for me. I could have gone there at any time. It's not your fault that I want it for both of us. I can't have it alone. We must share it."

"Thank you, my dear."

Katharine shrugged her shoulders. "It's time I was preparing the evening meal. It will be ready in about an hour."

Luther remained silent, and Katharine put a hand on his shoulder. "Someday, dear husband, you and I will have peace and happiness together. Someday we'll rest."

Luther put a hand over hers. "You're a wonderful wife,

my Lord Kate, and I love you with my whole heart and do not want to leave you, but I truly want the Lord Jesus to remove my soul into His care. I am ready to go. I have lived out and finished the course assigned to me by God."

Katharine drew her hand away. "You don't know that you have finished the course."

"You're right," Luther sighed. "God alone knows it."

Katharine left the room, and when she had closed the door behind her, she stood in the empty hallway, her face covered with her hands. "Dear God," she prayed, "let me keep him a little longer, please." Then she smoothed her hair and walked briskly down the stairs.

Luther went to Eisleben near the end of January, and Katharine felt the loneliness more than ever before. During the long winter months she felt increasingly restless. Luther had been gone before, even for long months at a time, but never had she felt so lonely. The boys had gone with their father, and only Margaret, now twelve, remained with her mother in Wittenberg.

One afternoon Katharine was in the study, where she often sat because it made her almost feel the presence of her husband. In no other room in the parsonage did she feel as close to him as she did in his study. She walked to the wide window and stood watching the snow falling. Margaret came in and put an arm around her mother's waist.

"Margaret, I have never before been so lonely for your father."

Margaret tossed her head. "O Mother, that's probably because Father and the boys both are gone. You miss them all."

Katharine continued to stare out at the falling snow. "Perhaps," she answered. "But I can't seem to still my fears, and I pray that God will bring them home soon."

Margaret said, "Isn't the snow beautiful, Mother?"

"Yes, it's beautiful, Margaret, but—"

"But what, Mother?"

Katharine impatiently brushed away a tear. "It's so cold, so terribly cold. I pray for spring to hurry. Your father gets so cold."

Margaret put her cheek against her mother's wet one. "Mother dear, I'm here. I'll stay with you and will be company for you. And besides, God will take care of Father. He is everywhere with him."

Katharine smiled. "You are a dear child. I am so happy that I have you, and you are a lot of company for me."

Early in February Katharine received a long cheerful letter from Luther and felt better for days afterward. Several more letters came during the next two weeks, reporting on his health and on the progress in the attempt to reconcile the two Counts of Mansfeld.

Then, finally, Katharine received the letter she was praying for. "Margaret!" she cried, "Margaret! Wolf! Where is everyone?"

Margaret and Wolf came running to her. "What is it, Mother? What's happened?"

Katharine put her arms around her daughter and smiled at Wolf. "O Margaret," she said weakly through her tears, "your father's coming home. He's coming home!"

A few days before Luther was to arrive, Katharine saw Pastor Bugenhagen coming up the walk. His shoulders were rounded, and his head hung down. A few minutes later, in Luther's study, Katharine greeted him, "Pastor, it's good to see you."

Pastor Bugenhagen looked at her and then quickly looked away.

Katharine continued: "I suppose you've heard that Doctor Luther is coming home," she said. "I'm so happy. I've missed him."

"Katharine," Pastor Bugenhagen interrupted, "I have something to tell you."

The sound of his voice and the expression on his face stopped Katharine. She stood looking at him, waiting for him to continue.

Pastor Bugenhagen swallowed. "Our beloved doctor is dead," he announced. "He died in Eisleben on February 18." He spread his hands and stared at the floor. "They are bringing him home. He will be here Monday, the 22nd."

Katharine didn't say anything. She stood opposite the pastor, looking at him. Finally Pastor Bugenhagen asked, "Is there anything I can do?" Katharine shook her head, and the pastor turned and left the room.

As soon as he had left, Wolf entered the study. Katharine looked at him. "Wolf, our dear doctor is gone?" She put it in the form of a question. Wolf ducked his head and asked, "Can I do anything for you, Mistress Luther?"

She looked at his red-rimmed eyes, his hands twisting and untwisting. "No, Wolf," she answered. "Just see that I'm alone for a few minutes, please."

"Yes, Mistress Luther, I'll see to it." Wolf answered and left the room.

Katharine walked to Luther's desk and sat at it, running her fingers over the scarred top. "Why aren't there any tears?" she wondered. She said over and over to herself, "The doctor is dead." It just couldn't seem to get through, to seem real. She looked up and saw the sunlight filtering in through the window. She remembered back to the day when she had first arrived in Wittenberg. How she had hated the sight of the

141

dusty streets and the shabby buildings! She smiled when she remembered how she had feared that Luther would never love her. Now, after twenty-one years of marriage, she was certain of his love. Hans was almost twenty, Martin fifteen, and Paul thirteen. Her smile faded when she thought of baby Elizabeth, who was now little more than a soft, sweet-smelling memory, and little Lena, who lived in Katharine's heart as brightly as ever. "So many have gone," she thought. "And now my dear doctor is gone, and I'm alone."

On Monday, February 22, 1546, Luther's body was brought through the Elster Gate and into Wittenberg. Throngs crowded the streets following the procession to the Castle Church. Immediately behind the hearse, in a carriage, Katharine rode with some of the distinguished women of the church. Following her in another carriage rode the Luther children.

Later, Katharine sat in the dim coolness of the church and listened to Pastor Bugenhagen speak from the pulpit. When he had finished, she saw Melanchthon slowly walk to the pulpit. When he spoke, she raised her eyes and listened to him.

"Luther was too great," Melanchthon said, "too wonderful for me to depict in words. If there ever was a man on earth I loved with my whole heart, that man was Luther. One person is an interpreter, one a logician, another an orator, affluent and beautiful in speech, but Luther was all in all — whatever he wrote, whatever he uttered, pierced to the soul, fixed itself like arrows in the heart — he was a miracle among men."

As Melanchthon talked of his beloved friend, Katharine sighed and wondered why there were still no tears. "I'm empty," she thought, "too empty for tears."

142

As Luther was buried at the foot of the pulpit, Katharine watched and felt detached from the proceedings. After the service she started blindly for home. She felt a strong arm helping her and dimly realized that it was Melanchthon.

At home she found her children in the great front room crying, trying to comfort one another. She stood in the door-way. "Children! Your father would not want you to weep so."

Hans ran to her, his handsome face streaked with tears. "O Mother," he cried, "Father is gone!"

Katharine put her arm around her son, and the other children gathered around her. She had listened to learned men in the church talk about the great Reformer, Dr. Martin Luther, and there had been no tears. She had seen the people of his congregation weeping and mourning the loss of their pastor, and she had found no release. Now, as she looked into the tear-streaked faces of her children and heard Hans say, "Father is gone!" she felt the hot tears stinging her eyes. Soon she, too, wept freely. In a few minutes, however, she controlled herself and talked to the children calmly. "Remember, children," she told them, "Father always had a comforting word for us in times like this."

They looked into her eyes. Then Margaret said softly, "Yes, Mother. God will take care of us. He is everywhere with us."

$\mathcal{L}$IFE IN GOD'S INN, the Lutheran parsonage of Wittenberg, continued, but with a great difference. When Luther was alive, life rushed on like great waves continually building up and splashing down. Now for Katharine and her children it flowed like a sluggish stream. They all made a great effort to comfort one another, to keep within their hearts a purpose for living. The children looked forward to their futures and made plans, but Katharine worked only because of them. For herself she felt that life was over. Her only purpose, her only happiness now was her children.

One day, some weeks after Luther's funeral, Katharine entered the kitchen and found Margaret sweeping the floor. "Margaret, what are you doing?" she asked.

Margaret stopped working and looked at her mother with a new, grown-up look. "I want to help. Now we must all work together, help one another."

"Thank you, dear Margaret," Katharine said. She looked away as Margaret again wielded the broom. "Where are the boys?" she asked.

"They're outside, helping Wolf. He doesn't feel very well today."

After Katharine had eaten and helped Margaret clean the room, she threw a shawl over her shoulders and went outside. She found Hans and Martin and Paul working with the live-stock. "Boys," she cried, "where's Wolf?"

Hans stood straight and put an arm around Katharine. "He's not feeling well, Mother. We're doing his work for him."

"Where is he, Hans?"

"He's in his cottage, lying down. Been there all morning. He told us not to disturb him."

Slowly Katharine picked her way down the path to Wolf's cottage and went in. "What's wrong?" she asked.

He turned his old, sad face to her. "Mistress Luther, I am ready to die."

"No, Wolf, please. Don't talk that way. You are not ready to die." She started for the door. "I'll get the physician. We'll take care of you, Wolf."

His quiet, firm voice stopped her. "I want to go, Mistress Luther. I want to join the doctor."

Katharine felt it was hopeless, but she sent for the physician. She and the children were standing outside when Dr. Schurf came out of Wolf's cottage. He looked at their anxious faces and shook his head. "He's dying," he told them.

They did all they could for Wolf, but it was of no avail. He lay in his bed not moving, uncomplaining. In a short time he died peacefully in his sleep. Katharine comforted the children, for they had loved Wolf. "He is with his beloved doc-tor," she told them. "Do not mourn too much for him."

Katharine missed Wolf and often wished in the days that followed his death that he were still with her and the chil-dren, but somehow it seemed right that, with Doctor Luther gone, Wolf should be gone too. He had been a part of the doctor's life for so long — longer than she had, and Wolf without his "good Sir Doctor" was incomplete.

The months following Luther's death were black days, and Katharine was astonished at the events that followed. Many lies were circulated concerning the great Reformer's death, and many people turned their backs on his widow and children. Katharine found this difficult to understand, but in her grief she could do nothing but try to care for her children as best she could. However, they needed money. She owned property and many fine possessions, but there wasn't enough money. She finally realized that something would have to be done. In the meantime she and the children stayed on in the Black Cloister.

One evening they were all in the study, the boys sitting at a table discussing their future. "I'm going to be a lawyer," Hans stated, "and nothing is going to stop me."

Paul leaned back. "And I'll be the greatest physician Germany has ever seen. Counts and kings and nobles will demand my services."

The boys looked at Martin, who hadn't said a word. "What about you, Martin?" Paul asked. "What will you be?"

Martin glanced at his mother. "You know what I'll be," he said softly, "a pastor, like Father. That's what he said I'd be just a few minutes after I was born."

Katharine looked up from her sewing. "Is that what you want, Martin?" she asked.

Martin's answer was quiet and firm. "Yes, Mother, it is exactly what I want."

Hans rose then and slapped Martin on the shoulder. "Come on, let's build a roaring fire in the fireplace."

As the boys heaped the wood high, Katharine watched them with pride. When the fire cast a rosy glow on the room, they all settled down to a few relaxed minutes before going to bed. The clatter of horses' hoofs startled them, and Hans ran to the door. Now that Luther was gone, they had few visitors, and they were excited about an unexpected one. Hans returned with Katharine's brother, Hans von Bora. Katharine threw herself into his arms. "Hans, it's so good to see you. I've felt so alone," she cried.

The children chorused, "Alone? With us here?"

Katharine drew away from her brother and smiled. "I'd have gone out of my mind without you, my dear children, but I've felt the need of a man to advise and help me."

Hans settled himself comfortably before the fire, his long legs stretched in front of him.

"Katharine," he said finally, "how are you getting along?"

Katharine folded her hands in her lap and stared at the fire. "Not very well," she answered. She told him of what had happened since Luther's death and how most of the citizens of Wittenberg had deserted her. "I don't understand it," she said, "for some reason they feel hostile toward me. I felt that as Dr. Luther's widow I would be treated fairly and with respect. But —" She spread her hands in a helpless gesture. "I simply don't understand it," she finished.

Hans strode in front of the fire. Finally he stopped in front of Katharine. "Would you like me to stay here for a while as your adviser? Perhaps as a man and as your brother I can accomplish something for you."

Katharine was profuse in her gratitude and told him over and over how good it was to have him there to help her. She went to bed that night feeling more secure and safe and feeling more promise for the future than she had since Luther's death.

The next morning Hans was up early. After breakfast he and Katharine went into Luther's study while the children did the chores. "Now, Katharine, where shall we start?" Hans asked.

Katharine wrung her hands. "Hans, I don't like to say this, but we do need money. The dear doctor provided for us in his will, but it seems that we cannot get the money."

"Have you asked the chancellor about this?"

"Yes. He says the doctor's will is not legal. The dear doctor thought he had provided well for his widow and children, but the chancellor puts me off when I try to talk to him about money."

"How often have you gone to him?"

Katharine hung her head. "Only once, I'm afraid. I went to him, fully confident of his help. When he treated me as he did, I was so utterly embarrassed that I couldn't force myself to go again."

Hans shook his head. "You can't let your pride stand in the way. I'll go down to the chancellor right now and see that you get some money." He picked up his coat. "Also, I'll look into the details of Luther's will." He stopped. "What about Melanchthon and Bugenhagen?" he asked.

Katharine shook her head. "They have been unable to do anything for me."

When Hans reached the door, Katharine went to him and laid a hand on his arm. "Hans, there is something else."

Hans turned to her, his eyebrows raised.

"It's important to me," Katharine continued. "Will you ask the chancellor if I may talk to him soon?"

Hans took her hand in his. "Of course I will, Katharine. I'll see to it."

As Katharine watched her brother go down the road, she said, "God be praised!"

148

Hans accomplished what Katharine could not. Luther's will was declared legal, and a promise of a monthly allowance was made. Then, under pressure, the chancellor also grudgingly consented to see Katharine. A few days later she and Hans were seated across from the chancellor in his office. The chancellor leaned back and folded his hands on his stomach. He looked at her through squinted eyes. "What is it you want to talk about, Mrs. Luther?" he asked.

Katharine glanced at Hans and shifted uneasily in her chair. She swallowed and lifted her chin. "I want to buy Wachsdorf."

The chancellor leaned forward. "You mean the estate that joins Zulsdorf?"

Katharine nodded.

The chancellor was obviously annoyed. "That property is no good," he said, "absolutely no good. It floods every year in the spring. Why on earth do you want it?"

Katharine lowered her head. "I intend someday to live at Zulsdorf. I'll sell the parsonage, and the children and I will make Zulsdorf our home. We'll need Wachsdorf too."

The chancellor drummed his fingers on the desk. "Your husband wouldn't have approved of this, Mrs. Luther."

Katharine's head shot up. "On the contrary, he intended to purchase Wachsdorf someday. He liked the property very much."

Hans reached over and took one of his sister's hands. "Are you positive that you want it, Katharine?" he asked. "It really isn't a very desirable piece of property, you know."

Katharine's eyes were wide as she answered her brother. "The dear doctor wanted it for the children."

The chancellor stood. "No!" he nearly shouted. "I will not give my permission for you to buy that worthless property. I am responsible for the way you spend every bit of the money

149

that Dr. Luther left you in his will, and I will not approve this foolish expenditure."

Hans stood also. "Dear sir," he said softly, "I really believe that it would be best for you to take a few days to consider this small request of Mrs. Luther's." He looked into the chancellor's eyes. "Don't you think so?"

The chancellor returned Hans's gaze, then looked away. "Very well. I'll give Mrs. Luther my answer in a few days."

As they walked toward the parsonage, Katharine held her brother's hand. "I won't get Wachsdorf, Hans. He won't let me buy it."

Hans smiled. "Just wait, Katharine. I think his answer will be yes. Just wait and see."

A few days later the chancellor came to the parsonage. "Mrs. Luther, against my better judgment I am going to allow you to buy Wachsdorf."

Katharine thanked him and said that she and Hans would attend to it immediately. The chancellor then put his hands behind his back. "I am responsible for what happens to you, Mrs. Luther, and I feel this great responsibility deeply. I feel it my duty to advise you concerning your children."

Katharine stiffened. "What about my children?"

"What are they doing?"

"Doing? What do you mean?"

"I mean, are they being educated?"

"Paul is studying to be a physician, Martin is studying theology, and Hans is studying law. Surely you know all this."

"Yes," he admitted. "I do know. What about Margaret?"

"Margaret is only thirteen years old," Katharine snapped.

The chancellor rubbed his hands together thoughtfully. "Mrs. Luther, I beg your forgiveness, but I do not feel that you are capable of giving your sons the proper training."

"I don't understand."

"The boys still have a few years of study. That takes money. Paul is only fourteen, and he has quite a number of years before he can support himself, and Margaret is a helpless girl of thirteen." He spread his hands and raised his eyebrows as if to say, "See how hopeless it looks?"

"What do you propose I do with my children?" Katharine asked.

"Why, I believe they should all be put into the homes of people who can give them a good start in life. I'm interested only in their welfare. I feel that we should do all in our power to see that the sons of Dr. Luther receive proper training."

Katharine clenched her fists at her sides and tried to control her anger. "You may take everything I own. You may take my money, my home, my property, but you will not take my children!"

The chancellor sighed. "You make things so difficult for me, Mrs. Luther. Believe me, I am only trying to do my best for your sons."

"I'm sorry," Katharine said finally, "I'm afraid I've offended you. It's just that I'm trying to the best of my ability to take care of the doctor's children as he would want me to." She hesitated, then continued, "Will it be all right if I talk to Melanchthon and Cruciger and get their advice on this?"

The chancellor agreed and left the house. The next day Katharine talked to Melanchthon and Cruciger, and they agreed to speak to the chancellor on her behalf. A few days later, she was informed that the matter was settled and her sons could stay with her.

151

Shortly after this she called her children into the study. She told them what had happened. "We don't have much," she said, "but we can manage. We can buy Wachsdorf, and soon we'll sell the parsonage and go there to live."

Margaret clung to her mother. "We'll raise vegetables and fruit and pigs and chickens, and we'll net fish. Mother, we'll get along at Zulsdorf. We'll be happy there."

Katharine patted her hand. "How often I said that to your father! I used to say, 'Dear Doctor, we'll be happy at Zulsdorf.'" She shook her head. "We never got there."

"We'll get there this time, Mother."

Katharine straightened. "I'll sell the parsonage and whatever else I can. The money will be used for the boys' education. I think we can manage, children. Now, go along and tell Uncle Hans to come in here. He's going home in a few days, and we've got plenty to do."

Katharine and her children made plans to leave Wittenberg. As far as Katharine was concerned, they couldn't leave soon enough. Then something happened to delay their plans. Emperor Charles V tried to destroy the effects of Luther's labors. The defensive measures of the Protestants only fanned the flame that was Charles's anger. The Emperor, however, played a double game. He was false both to the Pope and to the Protestants. He sought only power for himself. In Germany he won the aid of the Duke of Bavaria by promising him he would be made an elector. Others bit on the attractive bait he held out to them. There were some that betrayed the Protestant faith. Slyly, cleverly, the Emperor worked, until he had an army of nearly fifty thousand men in upper Germany.

Katharine listened to the rumble of fear trembling through Wittenberg and she decided to go to Magdeburg for the safety of her children. She told them to dress warmly, and she herself put a few of their belongings in a chest.

In a few hours they stepped out into the street. Paul and Hans carried the chest and preceded them down the street. Everywhere people were shouting and rushing up and down the streets. Twice Katharine was almost knocked down. Whenever they saw a man with a cart or a carriage and horses, they begged him to take them to Magdeburg. Each time they received a gruff refusal.

Finally, near the edge of town, a man with a cart said they could climb in if they hurried. Thankfully Katharine helped the children put the chest into the cart, and they climbed up. The driver drove the horses like a mad man, constantly whipping them and yelling in coarse, crude language for them to go faster, faster. The roads were rough, and it was getting very dark. Katharine and her children huddled together in the cart during the wild flight. Finally the horses stopped and refused to go on.

"My horses are exhausted. You'll have to find your own way from here," the driver said.

Katharine thanked him and climbed out of the cart and motioned to the children to follow.

They stood by the side of the road in the darkness. No one spoke. It started to rain, and Katharine broke open the chest and told each of them to take as much as he could carry. Then, through clenched teeth, she said, "Let us go! We are in God's care. He will not forsake us."

The weary family started down the road toward Magdeburg. They had walked for what seemed an endless time when they came to a house. "We'll knock," Katharine said, "and see if they will take us in for the night." When the door opened in answer to her knock, Katharine gasped. Melanchthon stood in the doorway! His cart, he explained to her, had turned over in a ditch, and he had stopped at this house for shelter. The peasants who lived in the house, after being told who Katharine was, were happy to give them shelter.

After a warm meal and a night's sleep the peasant drove them to Magdeburg. In that town Katharine found friends. George Major, a professor of theology and a friend of Luther, took her to a senator's home. The senator and his wife were happy to receive the Luther family and begged them to live with them. Katharine was happy to agree, and the family settled down.

The peace and happiness lasted only a few days. Katharine knew they couldn't stay indefinitely in Magdeburg. She knew it wasn't safe yet to return to Wittenberg or to try to get to Zulsdorf. Finally she decided that the safest place to go would be Denmark. The next morning she suggested this to the senator.

"No, Mrs. Luther," he replied, "I don't see any sense at all in such a move."

Katharine insisted. She felt sure they would be safe once they reached Denmark. Eventually the senator gave in and took them, against his will, to Brunswick. There he begged Katharine to change her mind and turn back. "No," she replied, "I am sure we'll be safe in Denmark."

In Brunswick they hired a wagon and continued on their journey. On the road they saw troops carrying the colors of the Emperor. Katharine was alarmed and begged the driver to hurry to the next town, Gifhorn. When they reached Gifhorn, she heard rumors about troops and how they were marching all over in every direction. She found it impossible to find lodging. With a sigh she turned to the driver. "It's too dangerous to try to continue to Denmark. Turn back."

On the way back, not knowing where they were going, they stopped at an inn to eat. When they were seated and had

154

been served, they heard a man at another table talking about Wittenberg. Katharine immediately rose and went over to his table. "I'm from Wittenberg," she said. "Do you have news of what happened there?"

The man smiled. "Yes, ma'am. Wittenberg fared well after all. Too bad about Lucas Cranach, the famous artist, though."

"Lucas?"

"Yes, do you know him?"

She nodded, and the man continued. "Lucas heard that Elector John Frederick was captured at Muehlberg, and he went personally to the Emperor's tent on the battlefield and pleaded for Frederick's release."

"What happened?" Katharine asked.

The man shrugged his shoulders. "His request was refused. But," he added, "Lucas Cranach remained, a voluntary prisoner."

"Lucas is a great man," Katharine said.

The man nodded in agreement.

"What happened to the Castle Church in Wittenberg?" she asked now. "And Doctor Luther's grave, what happened to that?"

The man took a bite of food. "Well, it seems that the Duke of Alva wanted to dig it up, and he yelled that he was going to scatter the archheretic's ashes to the four winds, but the Emperor stopped him. He said, 'I make war with the living, not the dead.'"

Katharine thanked him and returned to her table. "Hurry and finish eating," she told the children. "We're going back to Wittenberg."

When they arrived in Wittenberg, Katharine took the children first to the church. Inside, they knelt at Luther's grave at the foot of the pulpit and thanked God for His mercies.

155

In the parsonage they found that the soldiers had had brutal and savage revenge. Nearly all of the furniture had been smashed, the walls were spattered, and most of their food and wine was gone. Katharine and the children roamed from room to room in astonished silence. Finally Katharine straightened her shoulders. "Let's get some rest now," she said. "We have a lot of work to do in the morning."

Margaret turned to her mother. "What do you mean, Mother?" she asked. "Are we going to — "

Katharine interrupted her. "We'll have to restore the parsonage. We'll begin tomorrow."

chapter twenty

*N*ow THE LUTHER FAMILY had less than ever. Food was scarce, and they all wore clothes that had been patched many times. Most of what Katharine had owned that was of any value had been stolen or destroyed, but she didn't complain. She and the children worked hard to restore the parsonage to a semblance of its former appearance, and as long as they had clothes to wear, even though patched, and food to eat, though not quite enough of it, and a home to live in, though it was nearly a shambles, she believed God was with them and would not permit them to suffer beyond what they could endure. To her children, at devotions and prayers, she imparted this faith. They worked through each day with lighthearted spirits and pleasant, smiling faces. If any of them did start to indulge in self-pity, Katharine would remind them, "God is not dead! He lives!" And the pouting face would be wreathed in smiles.

One evening after devotions Hans turned to his mother. "I've been wondering," he said, "about what I should do now."

"What do you mean, son?"

"Well, I've finished my studies here in Wittenberg, and I don't want to just sit around doing nothing."

Katharine smiled. "What would you like to do, Hans?"

Hans laughed. "I'd like to continue my studies, go to Königsberg University."

"Then you shall go."

"Mother, let's be sensible," he said. "You know that I can't go on. We don't have the money."

"I said you'll go to Königsberg University, Hans, and I meant it. Now all of you go to bed. It's late."

They left the room, and Hans, at the door, said, "Mother, aren't you going to bed too?"

"Yes, dear, in a few minutes. We'll talk in the morning about when you are to leave for the university."

After they had gone, Katharine went to a little niche in the wall behind the fireplace. She brought out the goblet she had hidden so long ago. The firelight cast a glow that made its crystal loveliness shimmer in the half light. There were tears in her eyes as she looked at it. She remembered when Luther had wanted to give it to Agricola and how later he had chided her for hiding it. "I'm going to sell it," she thought now. "It will bring enough to send Hans to Königsberg."

A few days later Katharine silently packed a knapsack for Hans. He was dressed for traveling, walking around the kitchen in heavy, unfamiliar boots. "These boots are awkward, Mother," he said.

"They will hold up. That's why I bought them. You have many miles to walk."

Hans came to her side. Gently he took the piece of cheese she was slicing and put it on the table. He held her in his arms. "Mother, thank you. Thank you so very much," he said.

158

Katharine clung to her son and fought the threatening tears.

Hans held her at arm's length. "How did you manage it, Mother?" he asked.

She turned away and put the cheese into the knapsack and began slicing pieces of bread. "Never mind how I did it; it's done."

Hans smiled. "I'd call it a miracle."

"Yes, we'll call it a miracle."

Later, as Hans stood in the doorway ready to leave and Paul and Martin and Margaret had said good-by, Katharine put a hand to his face. "Dear son," she said, "be careful. And remember your father's words, 'God will take care of you. He is everywhere with you.'"

Hans kissed her. "I'll remember, Mother. I'll never forget."

Katharine watched as her son walked down the road. She watched until he turned a corner and she couldn't see him any longer.

War had laid waste a large section of the country. Wearily the peasant ploughed his fields, knowing that others would reap the fruit of his toil. Katharine's thoughts reverted to Zulsdorf. Her husband had found another resting place, but she had not been permitted to bring comfort to her husband's declining years. They had also been denied a few last years together at Zulsdorf. Now, in her widowhood, the care of her children made staying at Zulsdorf impossible. They were very poor, and the high taxes took everything she had. Several months after Hans left for the university Katharine went to Dr. Bugenhagen. "Pastor, please help me. We need money for the bare necessities of life," she pleaded.

Dr. Bugenhagen patted her hand. "The chancellor will give you nothing?"

Katharine shook her head.

"What about some of the citizens of Wittenberg? Doctor Luther was their pastor, and he did a great deal for many of them. Won't any of them help?"

Katharine choked back her tears. "They have all turned their backs on me."

Dr. Bugenhagen sighed. "Katharine, I can help you, but only a very little. What else can I do?"

"I wondered if perhaps you would write to the King of Denmark. I feel sure that if he knew the circumstances of Luther's widow and children he would help."

Bugenhagen brightened. "Of course!" he said. "He will be distressed when he hears of this. He will help." He led Katharine to the door. "Go home now. I'll send a letter today. It won't be long now."

The King of Denmark did send her money, enough for the Luther family to live on. However, Katharine needed money to restore the parsonage and the grounds, and she was determined to do all she could in this direction. One day she called the children to her. "I've given our situation very careful thought," she told them, "and there is just one thing left for us to do."

"What's that?" Margaret asked. "Are we going to Zulsdorf?"

Katharine shook her head. "No, we can't go yet, because we can't sell the parsonage in its present state, and I won't leave until it has been restored. The people haven't gotten over the war yet; they have no money with which to buy property. No, we'll take in boarders. That will bring us enough money to get by."

160

"But, Mother, what do you know about taking care of boarders?" Paul asked.

Katharine laughed. "Son, for most of the twenty-one years that I was married to your father I ran a boardinghouse. The citizens of Wittenberg called the parsonage 'God's Inn.' The only difference now will be that we'll get paid for it." She looked at each of them. "You'll all have to help, however."

That night, as she lay in bed, Katharine prayed for strength and guidance. Then she did something she had been doing since her husband's death. She "talked" to him. She knew she couldn't actually talk to the dead, of course; it was just her way of thinking, of feeling her husband's presence. She had discussed things with him for so many years, it was almost a habit. "Dear Doctor," she whispered now into the darkness, "do you think this is a wise move? I can cook and clean. That's all I know how to do. Thanks to you, I have had years of experience in taking care of a house full of people. Dear Doctor, until I can be with you again, your children will be taken care of. I'll do it somehow, with God's help."

During the next few weeks a great change came over the parsonage. The long dining room was again filled at mealtime with students and men and women. Katharine and Margaret hurried between the table and the kitchen bringing large platters of food and taking away the empty dishes. After the meals they cleared the tables and washed the dishes. Then, while Margaret began preparing for the next meal, washing vegetables and cleaning fish or chicken, Katharine cleaned the rooms and aired the bedding. The boys, after their studies, did the heavy work and took care of the gardens and livestock. Often Katharine would look longingly at the garden and wish she could again be out there, her hands in the soil, the sun warming her body.

Dr. Bugenhagen came over one day. "Katharine, I'm sorry you have to do this."

161

"It's all right, Pastor. It's a means of staying alive, and it keeps me busy."

He looked at her. "My dear Katharine, I've just noticed how tired and pale you look. Are you ill?"

Katharine brushed a stray lock of hair from her eyes. "I'm not ill. I'm very tired, and I think I've lost some weight, that's all."

Dr. Bugenhagen shook his head. "You'd better take better care of yourself. Get more rest."

Katharine tossed her head impatiently. "I have to be up before dawn to start breakfast for the boarders. I cook three large meals a day, I clean the rooms every day. I can't possibly get to bed early at night," she laughed bitterly. "And you casually tell me to get more rest. I don't see how I can manage that!"

Dr. Bugenhagen apologized. "I'm sorry, Katharine, I —"

"Oh, pastor, forgive me. I'm tired, and I didn't know what I was saying. Please forgive me."

A few days later Katharine awoke with a headache. She called Margaret. "Send one of the boys for the physician. Quickly!"

The doctor came and felt her feverish head and turned to Margaret. "I don't know what it is, but she's a very sick woman. I imagine she's just been working too hard and is too thin."

Margaret took one of her mother's hands. "Her hand is so hot," she said.

"She has a high fever."

Margaret turned anxiously to him. "What can I do?"

"Keep her in bed, Margaret. She needs rest. Also, make her eat so that she'll get her strength back. Give her a little

162

warm beer several times a day. Your mother is over fifty years old and can't stand what she did fifteen or twenty years ago. She needs rest."

Margaret looked worried. "I'll do all I can, Doctor, but I wonder whether we'll be able to do everything alone. We have a lot of boarders."

"Must you keep the boarders?" the doctor asked.

Margaret nodded emphatically.

"Then hire a maid. That's all you can do. I'll talk to Doctor Bugenhagen about it."

That afternoon Dr. Bugenhagen brought a young woman to the parsonage. "I told her she'd be amply paid," Dr. Bugenhagen told Margaret. "This woman should feel honored to help Doctor Luther's widow and children."

"Why?" Margaret asked.

"Because Doctor Luther, as her pastor, did a very great deal for her at one time. This is an opportunity for her to repay his kindness."

Margaret sniffed. "No one owes us anything because of Father. We'll pay her for her work, and I only hope she does her work well."

Dr. Bugenhagen smiled. "You're proud, Margaret. Just like your mother."

The maid was a good worker. She arrived at dawn every morning and took over all of Katharine's chores. If, once in a while, she scrimped on the cleaning or failed to air a bed or two, Margaret overlooked it.

A few weeks in bed, plus the food that Margaret made her eat, helped Katharine. Soon she was sitting up and asking Margaret to tell her how things were going. Margaret assured her that everything was fine and told her that the maid was working satisfactorily. "Not one boarder has left us, Mother," Margaret said, "in fact, we've added two."

Katharine was pleased and was persuaded to remain in bed. She asked Margaret one day to bring her sewing basket to her. "I'll do the mending while I'm here, until the doctor says I can get up."

Margaret brought the basket, and Katharine searched for her thimble. "My thimble — where is it?" she asked.

"No one has touched your sewing basket since you've been ill, Mother."

"My gold thimble is gone."

Just then they heard the maid going down the hall, singing. Katharine and Margaret looked at each other with the same thought.

"Perhaps you'd better do some investigating, Margaret. See if anything else is missing," Katharine said wearily.

In a short time Margaret returned. Her face was a picture of dismay. "I'm sorry, Mother."

"Other things are missing?"

Margaret nodded. "Not only that, Mother, but I discovered she's not been doing such good work after all. She's been very deceitful."

Katharine sighed. "That's the way we're treated on all sides. We should have expected it."

Seeing the look on her mother's face, Margaret broke into tears. "It's all my fault," she cried. "I should have watched her more closely."

Katharine held her arms out. "Come here, Margaret. It's not your fault. A sixteen-year-old girl is not expected to know how to deal with such people."

The maid was dealt with by Katharine and discharged. She didn't want to have her punished or reported, but only

164

get her out of the house. Paul said, "Mother, you should report her to the authorities."

Katharine shook her head. "No, Paul. I talked to her. She's in God's hands. We're rid of her. That's all I care about."

She got out of bed then and resumed work. She was weak, but the enforced rest had given her enough strength to continue.

Katharine heard that John Frederick, a staunch Lutheran ruler of Saxony, had been defeated and captured in the battle of Muehlberg. She remembered him as an ardent disciple of Luther, a loyal Christian, and a man who had always been interested in the University of Wittenberg. In fact, it had been under his leadership that the university had been reorganized and for the first time become truly Lutheran. When she thought of this great man and his courage, her own cross lost half of its weight.

In January Dr. Bugenhagen came to Katharine. "I have just learned that the King of Denmark has only recently heard of your situation, and is going to send more money." He knew, of course, that you were having a hard time, but he didn't realize until now the seriousness of it."

"I'm glad," Katharine answered.

Later she told Margaret, "If the King of Denmark sends us more money, we won't have to take in boarders."

Margaret sighed. "I hope he sends it, then. I don't mind work, Mother, but I *am* getting tired."

Katharine stroked her daughter's head. "Of course you are. You've worked hard making beds, scrubbing, doing chores to which you are not accustomed. You deserve a rest."

January and February were bitterly cold, and Katharine and her children worked hard. There were still many boarders to care for, and the renovation of the parsonage was a huge task yet to be completed. When March came and the snow and ice thawed somewhat, Katharine drew a breath of relief. Soon it would be summer, and they would all feel better. Summer would bring warmth and life, and they would be able to continue. During the first week in March Katharine received a warm, friendly letter from the King of Denmark. The packet also contained money. "God be praised!" she said.

$\mathcal{S}$PRING CAME, and one by one the boarders left. Many of the students were leaving anyway, and as she didn't need the income now, Katharine asked the others to find other places to live. When summer finally came, the Luther family enjoyed privacy again. With summer came also the dust that settled over the town and gave the roads and houses a dirty, gray appearance. The odors of garbage thrown into the street and the livestock that roamed the town were nearly overwhelming.

On one particularly hot day Katharine and the children sat under a pear tree, trying to escape the heat. "I think it's time we went to Zulsdorf," she said.

The children were excited. "Mother, let's go quickly."

"It will take a few days to make arrangements and to get ready."

Margaret snickered. "I know why you're so anxious to go, Paul."

Paul frowned, and Margaret said, "Because at Zulsdorf we'll be close to Torgau, and that's where Anna lives."

Paul chased Margaret across the lawn. "You keep quiet!" he shouted.

The next few days were filled with excitement and activity. They packed their belongings, and there was a lot of discussion as to what should be taken and what should not. Katharine decided to go to Dr. Bugenhagen and see if he would help her make arrangements to sell the parsonage. As she left, Paul called out to her, "Tell him we want a fair price, Mother."

"I'll see to that," Katharine answered. "You get on with the packing."

Paul laughed, and Katharine started down the road. As she walked toward Dr. Bugenhagen's house, she noticed that the streets were strangely silent and empty. "It's too hot for anybody to be outside," she thought absently. A dog barked and snapped at her heels. The sound echoed hollowly down the street. Dr. Bugenhagen met her at the door. "Isn't it terrible?" he asked.

Puzzled, Katharine asked, "Isn't what terrible?"

"The plague. Wittenberg's been struck with the plague again."

Slowly Katharine started back toward the parsonage. When she came to the church, she went inside. Kneeling at the foot of the pulpit, she made the sign of the cross and prayed. Afterward she sat in one of the pews for a few minutes. "Dear Doctor," she thought, "what shall I do? Every instinct within me cries to leave, to run away. You wouldn't run away, I know, and once I stayed with you." She put her face in her hands and felt tears seeping through her fingers. "O Doctor, must I stay this time? These people are not my flock; I am not their shepherd. I am only your widow, and these people have long ago turned their backs on me." She cried softly for a while and then brushed the tears away. "I am the widow of Doctor Martin Luther," she said aloud to the empty church. "I have a responsibility to his memory." Her

168

words echoed in the great church. She looked again at the spot where her husband was buried. "I will stay, dear Doctor," she said. "I dare not go!"

The plague brought more than physical suffering to the people of Wittenberg. It brought fear. Charity was a thing forgotten. Children fled from town, leaving their dying parents behind. Neglected bodies lay in the streets. The rumor went around that one could get rid of the plague by breathing on someone else and thus giving it to them. People forgot human decency. Children were seen trying to breathe on other children, even their parents, in order to get rid of the plague. Terror reigned in Wittenberg.

For five weeks Katharine and her children stayed in the parsonage, taking care of the sick, burying the dead, giving comfort to those who mourned their lost ones. The parsonage again looked like a hospital, and Katharine worked to the point of exhaustion every day and sometimes far into the night. There were many for whom she cared who only a short time before had refused to speak to her on the street. Some who had openly opposed her now felt her cool hand on their feverish brows. When they tried to thank her or to beg her forgiveness or to ask her in a puzzled tone, "Why are you doing this for me?" she merely smiled and told them to rest and laid a cool cloth on their heads. At the end of the summer, however, she was completely exhausted and could barely muster enough strength to carry her through a day. When she noticed how pale and thin Margaret was, she went to the physician.

"Doctor, do you think the plague is leaving now?"

The physician nodded. "It will be gone in a matter of days."

Katharine sighed with relief. "Do you think, then, that my children and I can leave?"

The doctor put a hand on her shoulders. "I think you'd better leave before you are all ill," he said. She smiled her thanks and started making preparations again to leave Wittenberg and go to Zulsdorf.

In a matter of days they were ready to leave. Katharine worked with feverish haste. "This time we'll make it," she said. At last the day came when they piled their belongings into the carriage and started toward Zulsdorf. Katharine rode through the Elster Gate without a backward glance. As they bounced along the rutted road, Paul smiled. "It will be good to be at Zulsdorf again," he said.

"Maybe Hans can come for a visit soon," Martin said.

They chatted happily, glad to be leaving Wittenberg at last and looking forward to living at their beloved Zulsdorf. After a few hours they settled into an amiable silence. Katharine watched the passing countryside and the changing fall colors with thoughtful eyes. She was thinking of all the things that had happened to her since Luther's death. She wondered how much longer she'd have to wait to join her dear husband.

Paul finally broke the silence. "I'll be a full-fledged physician soon, Mother."

Katharine smiled at him. "I know, son, and I'm proud of you. You did beautifully these past weeks during the plague."

Paul beamed. "The physician complimented me and said that I'll make a good doctor."

"I'm sure of it, Paul," she said.

Paul coughed and looked at the countryside. "I'll be glad when I am a physician and Anna and I will be married."

170

Katharine smiled. "Youth is always impatient," she said. "You and your Anna will be married in due time."

Margaret bounced on the seat. "O Paul," she said, "Anna is so pretty. The last time we went to Torgau I just looked and looked at her. You're so lucky to get her."

"I think she's lucky to get Paul too," Katharine said.

"Mother! Don't tell Anna that!" Paul laughed. They discussed wedding plans, and Paul said, "I wish you were ordained, Martin. Then you could marry us."

"I'll baptize your first child," Martin grinned.

"Martin! Let's not talk that way!" Katharine admonished him and glanced meaningfully at Margaret.

As they passed through a town, a dog rushed out and barked at the horses. One of them became frightened and reared on its hind legs. Katharine felt the carriage bumping, and she stood up to call to the driver. As she did, the carriage lurched, and she was thrown out. The driver managed to stop the horses, and the children ran to their mother. She lay in a puddle of water by the side of the road. Paul reached her first. Gently he lifted her head. "Mother, are you all right?"

Katharine opened her eyes. "I think so," she said, "but I'm not sure."

Carefully they helped her into the carriage. Her clothes were soaking wet, and the chill air penetrated to her skin. Paul wrapped her in a carriage robe and spoke to the driver. "Take us only as far as Torgau. We'll spend the night there."

By the time they arrived in Torgau Paul realized that his mother was very ill. They went to the home of Kaspar Grunewald, an old friend of the Luther family, and he welcomed them warmly. "I consider it a privilege to be able to help the widow and children of Dr. Luther," he said.

171

Katharine was put to bed, and a physician was called. After he had done all he could to make her comfortable, the physician turned to the children. "I've done all that I can. Keep her warm and see that she rests."

For weeks Katharine lay in bed. She was in pain, and the fever which burned inside weakened her. One night during the Advent season, when large flakes of snow were drifting to earth, she heard singing beneath her window. Margaret explained, "It's carolers from the church, Mother. They've come to sing Christmas carols for you."

Katharine smiled wanly. "Would you ask them if they know Dr. Luther's Christmas hymn 'From Heaven Above to Earth I Come'?"

Margaret left the room, and in a few minutes the carolers sang the beautiful hymn.

A smile crept over Katharine's flushed face. "Do you remember, Doctor?" she thought wistfully. "I had been busy all day, and I stormed into your study and asked whether it would be too much to ask you to hold the baby for a while. When I returned, you were rocking the baby and singing that song to her. You had composed that song for your child." Tears rolled down her cheeks as she remembered. She turned to Margaret. "It isn't a Christmas carol, I know, but do you suppose that they could also sing 'Ein' feste Burg'?"

Margaret nodded and left the room. As the words drifted up through her window, "A mighty Fortress is our God, a trusty Shield and Weapon," Katharine thought, "And do you remember how excited you were, dear Doctor, when you wrote that? Remember how we all had to sing it over and over so that we could lead the congregation in singing it?"

Through the haze that was slowly enveloping her, she

heard Margaret and Paul and Martin enter the room. She heard Margaret say, "I don't know, Paul. She thinks Father is here. She's talking to him."

She heard Paul say, "It's the fever. She's delirious."

Katharine could have explained. "I don't really talk to your father, it's just that I like to think of him, and my way is by 'talking' to him." She closed her eyes. She prayed silently. The children sat around her bed, their eyes wide in their pale faces. Once in a while they would look at one another wonderingly and then look again at their mother. Katharine prayed, and over and over she recited the Lord's Prayer and the Thirty-first Psalm. Once, after repeating the Psalm, she remembered that the doctor had made her learn it. In between her prayers she relived a great many things that had happened during their marriage, and once she gasped and then smiled and said, "My dear little Lena, my precious child."

The afternoon sun gradually faded, and only thin strips of light slanted into the room. Paul and Martin and Margaret sat in stunned silence. "Do you think Hans will get here in time?" Margaret whispered.

Paul shook his head. "I'm beginning to doubt it."

Then Katharine turned her head toward her children. "I'm very tired. Why don't you sleep too?" And she turned her face toward the wall.

After a few minutes Margaret rose. "I'll see if she's comfortable," she said. Paul and Martin watched her walk to the bed and lean over their mother. Then Margaret turned to them. "Mother's dead," she said. "She's at home with God."

Paul rose and took his sister in his arms. "Margaret," he said through his tears, "my little sister, don't cry. Remember what Mother and Father always told us: 'God will take care of you. He is everywhere with you.' "